Where It

Hurts

Jessica,
What a beautiful
person you are, on the
inside as well as the outside. I thank you & your
family for being so kind
to my son, Zachary.
May God's grace, love, &
mercies follow you all the
days of your lives.
Keep God Close,   Betty Jane
                        Dickson

Tell Me

Where It

Hurts

JANE DICKSON

TATE PUBLISHING & *Enterprises*

TATE PUBLISHING
& Enterprises

Tate Publishing is committed to excellence in the publishing industry. Our staff of highly trained professionals, including editors, graphic designers, and marketing personnel, work together to produce the very finest books available. The company reflects the philosophy established by the founders, based on Psalms 68:11,

"THE LORD GAVE THE WORD AND GREAT WAS THE COMPANY
OF THOSE WHO PUBLISHED IT."

If you would like further information, please contact us:
1.888.361.9473 | www.tatepublishing.com
TATE PUBLISHING & Enterprises, LLC | 127 E. Trade Center Terrace
Mustang, Oklahoma 73064 USA

Tell Me Where It Hurts

This title is also available as a Tate Out Loud product.
Visit www.tatepublishing.com for more information

This novel is a work of fiction. Names, descriptions, entities and incidents included in the story are products of the author's imagination. Any resemblance to actual persons, events and entities is entirely coincidental.

Cover design by Chris Webb
Interior design by Leah LeFlore

Published in the United States of America

ISBN: 978-1-6024706-5-1

07.03.21

DEDICATION

To God. For your absolute and unconditional love. For accepting me into your arms as I am. For giving me the ability to truely feel your great and powerful love at work in my life.

To my sons, Toby and Zachary. You are the treasures of my life. You both fill my heart with a deep and continuous love and joy. Never again will I be the same!

To my family. Thankyou!

To Lonnie. It is you, who is the true definition of what being a man is! Your unwavering love and support, even in time's when I wasn't quite so deserving, has lifted me up, to reach new heights.

Love, Betty

CHAPTER *one*

Sydney could see the edge of the small town that she had spent all of her young life, until leaving for college. As she neared the outskirts, it was for her, as if time had stood still. It was nearing dusk, with the thick dampness that threatened rain. The leaves were still hanging on with the last bit of life that they had, before another breeze would remove them from their home. All around she could see how slowly they wafted down, swirling as a ballerina would with a slow dance through the air, to a soft silent landing.

As she turned on the side street that would lead her to her childhood home, she spotted two small children running around chasing one another, without worry of the ominous clouds, or the whisper of the chill in the air, that winter always sent as a notice of its impending arrival. Their faces were smiling and free from all the cares of the world. Through her sealed vehicle, she could hear the excited scream of the one that was barely able to escape the fatal touch of the other child that would make them "it" and have to do the chasing.

Sydney's eyes started to fill up, thinking of Jeff that she left back in Colorado. She didn't expect him to be there when she returned from this trip. After all, she was venomous with her words to him before leaving and lethal with her anger. She and Jeff had always been best friends since their early teens. Even though their lives didn't have a lot of similarities, as far as the way they were both brought up, they really didn't have a lot of differences in their wounds. They both bled just as much as the other, they both felt the pain from their own sufferings, and they both were much wiser than other's their own age, from their tragedies.

But, the last episode had been the fatal and final blow that had brought both of them down to their knees and left them there. It was the death of their little boy, Jacob. This time there was none of the understanding between them that brought them closer, as did all the other pernicious memories they experienced. After Jacob's death, she needed to place blame, and Jeff being handy, was the one she tore at. She turned into something that was malicious, hateful, miserable, depressed, and so angry that it literally made her body tremble with its voracity, upon rearing its ugly head.

Sydney had carried a deep anger with her, from her mother's death. This anger had been with her for so long, that she wasn't even aware of it. What had started out as guilt from her mother's death somehow turned into anger, which was always just boiling beneath her surface. She spent her young years doing everything she could to show God how angry she was at Him. In doing this, her father also felt her wrath and tried to handle her as best as he knew how, but was always left unsure of himself. Sometimes he'd be too lenient, feeling that he couldn't be too awful hard on her after all she had been through. Then again, there were those few, but memorable, times in which he'd lost his temper with her and went to the other extreme. Those times weren't as often, but they did stop her behavior for a brief period of time. Sydney could always tell when he'd start to relax and then *off again* she'd go, taking him to the very edge of sanity and then the rollercoaster ride would once again start.

Sydney's father had died from a massive heart attack the year before, but before she could recover from the shock and horror of that, her son had been hit and killed instantly when he had spotted his mom getting out of her car across the street, while his day care provider, Tracy, was talking with another mother picking up her child. He had been standing right next to Tracy and as he spotted his mom, he moved with lightning speed out of Tracy's grasp and while running towards her, his face lit up with the biggest smile, while yelling "Hi Mommy!" all at the same time. Sydney realized he was barreling right towards her, without looking. She had suddenly felt as if she were moving in slow motion. She screamed, as she ran to stop the oncoming car from hitting her son. It was shear horror, watching the driver in his confusion, try to slow down, but not soon enough. He hit her little boy and watched his small body flip once through the air and hit the pavement with a resounding thud. As Sydney raced to his body, she knew, before she even felt for a pulse, that her little Jacob was gone.

It all happened so fast, that it left her reeling from the monstrosity of it all. She first went into her denial stage, pretending that nothing had changed. Then at the slightest tingling sensation of realizing that it wasn't some horrible nightmare came the depression that felt as if she were stranded in the middle of the ocean, trying not to drown from all of the waves that seemed to come more and more quickly, without giving her the time she needed to catch her breath. Jeff watched her decline, trying to pull her to shore, but she kept fighting him to where he knew that they both would drown, unless he let go. His own heart was shattered so badly, that some of those pieces of it were gone for good. He finally let go of her, he had his own battle of survival to deal with. His strength was zapped, his heart was crushed, his hope was diminishing with startling speed, and he still couldn't give up. He, too, had been through so much in his life, that to give up now was impossible for him to do. His survival mechanism kicked in, even when he didn't want it to. It seemed to have a will of it's own that wouldn't give him the option of choosing to quit. But survival didn't insure happiness, love, and the healing balm that his marriage needed so desperately, it only insured that he would get through it and that's all.

They became stranger's to each other, each turning inward to deal with their pain separately. Jeff turned to his work to get him through the endless hours till he could drop into bed with such exhaustion that he could finally shut the world out for a while. Jeff was working practically day and night, till he couldn't go anymore, then he'd go home. He felt like a walking zombie, so that when the call came in that Sydney needed to go back to their little town in Illinois to sign some papers from the sale of her father's home, he finally felt that this was a blessing. Not only would he be free from this tension that permeated the air with such thickness that it seemed to have made it difficult to even breath, but maybe this was finally the end. It was just another "issue" that he'd rather put off and ignore, than deal with right now, as he did with so many other things in his life. It had become a nice, tidy, comfortable pattern for him.

Even with the knowledge of what was making Sydney so hateful, he still intensely disliked this hateful being he had married. He felt as if she were trying to wipe away every single particle of love he had for her. It was as if she were scrubbing his heart with a wire scouring pad, till she rubbed the entire surface that held this love away, leaving a jagged, bloody gaping hole.

Sydney's memories floated back to just before they were

married. They had been considered girlfriend and boyfriend for four years, before Sydney finally hinted around that she thought that maybe they should split up. She told Jeff that she wanted more and that she didn't think he'd ever give her what she wanted. Sydney had held her poker face and didn't have a clue as to what she would do if he called her bluff, but as it turned out, her heart was right. He did love her and want to spend the rest of his life with her, but it took a slight nudge to get him to say it. She had never intended on leaving him, but she wanted to be married, to have children, to build a life together, without always wondering if he planned on staying with her, or if she would be like so many of her friends that dated one person for so long and all of the sudden, "poof," they were gone. They'd breakup, then be married to someone else before their own shadow was out the door of the one they left behind after so long.

Jeff finally proposed. He finally had enough guts to tell Sydney that he couldn't stand to think of not having her in his life. It was the most difficult thing he had ever had to do. He was not used to exposing his weaknesses and Sydney was one of them. So as hard as it was for him to show her his weakness, it was incredibly harder to let her out of his life or to imagine her with someone else. After weighing his choices, he caved. The night he proposed to her, he had become so overwrought with emotions that he actually cried, not knowing himself whether the tears were from his love for her or the fear of her saying no. Rather than looking vulnerable to Sydney by crying, she was moved beyond words. That night was the most intimate night that he could ever remember having with another human being. It was the intimacy they shared, not from a sexual standpoint, but emotionally. Finally, he had let go of his fear and in doing so they were able to touch the parts of their hearts that never would be nor could be touched in quite the same way.

CHAPTER *two*

Jeff wasn't a mean man, even though he had grown up with such an evil father, but he also knew when he wasn't loved and he wouldn't allow himself to ever have to go through that pain again. He had become a master at shutting down, at totally cutting out those who didn't give him the positive feelings that he liked to surround himself with. It wasn't as though he was able to make himself immune to the feelings of hurt or pain, but Jeff found that by totally shutting down, he was able to limit the dosage of pain that he would have to endure. Even though he was intelligent enough to know that it doesn't really work like that, he still would ignore it every time it reared its head. It would never vanish or go away, it was only being set aside, time and time again, until the day came that it would have to be faced up to and dealt with. Jeff wasn't planning on ever dealing with it; this way had become so much easier for him.

So as he sat there, slowly turning the pages of the photo album, he felt grief. He wanted to remember those happy times, with their smiling faces and love that shone brightly and abundantly. As he studied the one of Sydney in the hospital bed, holding their small little boy, she looked as though she were looking right through him from that picture. She had a beautiful expression on her face, a look Jeff never remembered seeing and wondering why he didn't notice it when he was taking her picture. Her eyes, even in the picture, held all the emotions that she was feeling. She was beautiful, with her hair disheveled and unruly and her face void of makeup, with the slight flush on her cheeks, and back again to those beautiful topaz colored eyes. Jeff rested the book on his lap as he leaned his head back on the couch, staring at the ceiling, hoping for some magical wand to bring everything back to what it used to be. Sitting in the silence of his living room, Jeff realized that he was feeling empty, a feeling totally devoid of emotions.

Sydney wiped the first tear away with the back of her hand. She tried with all her might to stave off the others that *always* followed, as if waiting for that particular tear to make the first move, before they would let themselves fall freely, as many rivers from their main source. Sydney wondered at how easily everything that she and Jeff had fought so diligently for collapsed as easily as a house of cards. She doubted that either one of them realized how little strength they really had, without one another to lean on. After all, who could blame a marriage that didn't withstand the death of their first child, not many did, at least according to the statistics.

As an RN, working in the ER and trauma units, Sydney had seen the faces that once held such confidence and smiles that were never hard to make, become stripped naked of their masks and show the grief, terror, fear, horror, and uncertainties that throw their normal lives into a tailspin, leaving them dizzy and unbalanced. How many times in college did her professors repeat how our lives can change in the blink of an eye, the toss of a coin, a split second and how, as being trained RN's, that they were going to have to think fast and logically. They could not allow anything to interfere with what is needed at that very moment. They had to be the calm, rational ones to handle the crisis at hand. Sydney was a pro. Her peer's admired how smooth Sydney always kept each situation.

When her son had his accident, Sydney had just finished a particularly long twelve hour shift at the hospital that was unusually busy. She'd had to deal with everything from a colicky baby whose mother seemed more in need of attention than the baby, judging from the dark circles underneath her eyes from lack of sleep, to an accidental gun shot wound, caused from a young man's friend while they were hunting. Jeff couldn't pick Jacob up that day, because he had a big trial and wasn't sure as to how late he would be.

Jeff had worked his way through college and struggled through law school. Nothing came easily for him, but on the other hand, nothing was impossible for Jeff either. When driven, he became almost a madman to attain something simply because he felt it was out of his reach. They had a life that ran smoothly. Every now and again, they'd have to iron out the kinks, but for the most part, they worked hard at their careers and respected each other's triumphs, while lifting one another up when they failed. Sydney had just finished college when they made the decision to be married, but Jeff still had four years or more to go. It was quite difficult for Jeff to carry a full load while working, but he never complained, just kept his eye on the target.

Sydney's father always told her how he always thought that the both of them would end up together. He said that he had always noticed a closeness between the two of them that most don't ever realize. So after they told him the news, he was worse than any mother could ever be. He started making arrangements, sitting with Sydney while picking out wedding invitations, and helping her to choose the colors. All the while, constantly pressing Sydney to get her wedding dress *before* the wedding, rather than after, on and on he went. Randy, her father's partner at the shop, even started getting in to the spirit of it all.

Sydney had to smile from the memories, it was comical to watch two grown men picking out the cake, speaking with the caterer's, ordering the flowers, and argue with each other, every single step of the way. Her only remorse was that her mother wouldn't be there to see her *big wedding day*. Though Sydney remembered her mother, sadly, through the years some parts of her memory faded. She had more love and attention than those with complete families. Sydney's father always told her that they had their own family. That they allowed those certain individuals, like Gretta, Randy and his wife Becky, into their lives, because they loved them as one loves a brother, sister, mother, or father, without *having* to love them because they were born into the same family. It was an advantage, her father often pointed out, that most didn't have the opportunity of having. They spent almost all of their free time with each other, because of their bond of friendship and love for one another.

It's not that Sydney or her father ever would have wished for their lives to have taken this direction, since the death of her mother. For they would have given anything to still have her, but in an ironic way, it put them both in the position of having to reach out for others. Something neither one of them would have done as easily if she were still alive. For Sydney, it removed some of her shyness from others. For her father, it gave him a chance to heal, to learn to treat each day with more gratitude and respect, and enjoy life a little more.

After Sally died, Charles learned a few things that he wished he would have learned before something so drastic happened. Everyone noticed his loss, including his daughter. He changed. It was as if a part of him died with Sally and the hole it left in his heart was planted with something subtly different. Charles still worked hard, but he managed his time in such a way that allowed Sydney and him plenty of time together. Finding that there were so many other aspects of life that he came to depend on, as much as he depended on the air he breathed. He couldn't understand how he had ever lived without it, for now his very mortality depended upon those moments. Work was still very important, but it was no longer *the* most important part of his life. Instead of work always being number one, it had drifted somewhere down the list, in its magnitude. Charles had been spending all of his time chasing after the *almighty dollar*, always thinking that it would give him more freedom. When in reality, it had taken away that very same freedom to enjoy the very things he worked so hard to attain. Charles was very private about expressing his feelings, but Sydney, even at that young age when her mother passed, could see something different in her father. At first it was a great, weary sadness in his eyes that were filled with guilt and regret. But those emotions seemed to change into something more intangible. He became more at peace, more understanding, more caring, and more balanced. It didn't happen all at once, it was a slow metamorphosis, hardly noticeable to anyone except for those close to him.

It wasn't until nine years after her mother's passing, that her father sat down with Sydney and had a nice long heart to heart talk with her. Sydney would never forget that day; it was the day before her graduation from high school. She remembered him looking so serious, that she felt a dread grip her that this wasn't going to be good.

Charles choked up as he began to speak to her, while they sat at the kitchen table. "Sydney, I can't begin to tell you how much I love you and how important you have been, are, and will be to me. I sometimes feel that I have to pinch myself that you're really my daughter, because of all your accomplishments.

I'm amazed at how well you've turned out, because at times, you've been quite adept at concealing it from me," he said with a chuckle, as Sydney smiled with embarrassment, knowing how difficult she had been at times.

"You are not only my daughter, but someone I have a great deal of admiration and respect for. I know how difficult it's been for you, but you somehow managed to wade through it all and still come out on top. Now tomorrow is not just your high school graduation, but the beginning of your adult life. You're going to college next year to find your own happiness. It's not going to be such a hardship for you as it will for me, but all the same it will be much different. You'll be making all of your own choices and with saying that, you must know that the choices that you decide to make will shape your life and point it in the direction in which they lead. So make 'good' choices, rather than bad, because I want you to have as powerful an impact on this world, as you have had on me." Charles paused.

"Unfortunately, it took me a long time to figure out the things that are really important in life. I don't know, maybe as I become older, I realize how petty some things that I used to worry about, have become so minute in the scheme of things, that they are hardly even noticeable to me anymore. Sydney, you've carried a lot of guilt with you through the years, sometimes I almost think that it's that guilt that's driven you so hard. You loaded yourself down with extracurricular activities, school, homework, and even took on a part time job with the little time you had left over. I know that you don't like to express your feelings, which you've probably inherited from me. But you cannot run from your feelings your whole life, by smothering them with work, activities, whatever, just so that at the end of the day, you're too tired to even think or allow yourself to feel." He raised his hand, as he watched her lips start to form a denial.

He knew her like a book; she was an identical image of her mother, except for her height and the quiet strength. Sydney, he knew, would gain her mother's "quiet strength" as she became older. It would become more polished and controlled. Sydney had the strength, he knew, but it was always speaking in loud volumes, rather than remaining hardly noticeable. He was positive that she had made it so evident to everyone on purpose, so as to ward off anyone thinking that she was reaching out for any sympathy. It was much easier for her to reject it, than to have to feel uncomfortable from it.

"I know that what I'm telling you today will be the last thing on your mind tomorrow. I just want you to hold my thoughts with you, whether you pull them out and use them or not. You and I have come down a hard road, it's been pretty bumpy at times, I know. I've found that in my life, most of the things that I missed were because I just simply wasn't looking for them. You know, when your mother died, that renewed my faith in God. It's odd, how He works. Sure I was angry with Him, but your mother changed all of that for me. Sally showed me that miracles really do happen. While I held your mother's hand as she took her last breath, I felt something amazing in the room. I can't explain it to you, but I do know that someday you will feel that same feeling I hope, because then you will truly begin to live."

CHAPTER *three*

So as Sydney drove down those old familiar streets, she felt a comfort, even through her sadness. As she rounded the last corner the light drizzle of rain began. As she pulled into the driveway, she stayed in her car and stared long and hard at her childhood home. Sydney sat there as if she were looking for evidence of all it had weathered throughout the years, but instead it stood proudly in front of her. Her home was just as beautiful and well maintained as if it were brand new. Sydney glanced over to Gretta's home next door, half expecting to find her on the porch awaiting her arrival, but sadly Gretta's home seemed to show the neglect that hers did not. The yard needed to be raked, weeds seemed to thrive, and it was in desperate need of a paint job. The house almost seemed to be overcome with sadness at losing Gretta's presence. Gretta had fallen ill and after her son's could no longer give her the medical care that she needed, they had no other choice but to place her in a home where she would have the constant care and medical attention that she needed around the clock.

Sydney placed her luggage up on the front porch and walked around the garage to retrieve the key. It seemed so odd to her to find that key in it's same hiding spot after so many years, but Randy and Becky had not changed a thing, except to make sure that the lawn was mowed and had a once a month cleaning on the inside.

As she opened the front door, she found that someone had placed fresh autumn colored flowers on the table that she used to throw her backpack and jacket after school, with an envelope propped up in front of them. For a split second she almost thought that they would be from Jeff, but after opening the card, she found Becky's handwriting on the inside. It read:

Dear Sydney,

I hope that you find everything in order. I've placed some boxes in the garage for packing. I stocked the fridge with some lunch meat, cheese, eggs, etc., in case you get hungry . . . I know how tired you must be from driving all the way from Colorado. Randy has a few guys to help load everything up once it's ready to be moved. I'm sorry that I couldn't be here to welcome you home this evening, but we've had an emergency at the shelter. I talked to Jeff earlier and he asked that you call him when you arrived. I think that he was concerned with you driving the whole way instead of just flying, but well . . . you know how men are, always thinking that we're incapable of doing anything on our own without them! Ha! Also, I don't want to wake you tomorrow morning, so why don't you give me a jingle when you're up and moving around. I've set aside a few days to come and help you pack. Besides, I'm excited to see you and visit with you! Get some rest. Love, Becky p.s. Randy just asked me to ask you if you could please call us when you arrive also. Another man!! Ha!

Sydney smiled; Becky was always so thoughtful and humorous at the same time. Always seeming to know when her humor was needed and constantly working at trying to keep everyone smiling and positive. Sydney supposed that in her line of work that's exactly what was needed.

After taking a walk through the house, finding nothing had changed, Sydney had suddenly felt ravenous as she opened the refrigerator door and found that Becky had somewhat gone overboard with the groceries. It was filled as if getting ready to feed a family of ten. Sydney realized that she had eaten next to nothing, while giving herself constant jolts of caffeine while driving. Her stomach seemed to reply, with its audible groan. So she pulled out the makings of a sandwich and grabbed a soda as she looked out the kitchen window over to where Gretta's beautiful garden used to be, but now was overgrown and barely visible. After finishing the last bite of her sandwich, she picked up one of her bags and slung it over her shoulder as she went upstairs to soak in a nice hot tub. The full tummy, warmth and steam from the bath, made Sydney slip into her old bed and fall asleep within seconds of hitting the pillow, forgetting to call Becky or Jeff.

The next morning, Sydney awoke with a start. It took a moment to realize where she was and as she looked outside, she found the same clouds still wallowing overhead with the attitude that they were going to stick around for a while. Only today, the rain was coming down pretty steadily. As she lay her head back on her pillow, she wished she could just go back to sleep for a while, but knew how much work there was ahead of her. The rain and clouds didn't do much to lift her mood either. After glancing at her watch and seeing that it was going on 9:30 a.m., decided that she had better get moving.

She remembered that she still needed to call Jeff and Becky, so after making a quick decision, decided to get the phone call with Jeff over with first. She dialed the office, knowing that's where he'd be at this time of the morning. After reaching his secretary and being told that he was in court, she felt relief and just asked the secretary to relay the message that she had arrived safe and sound.

"No, Rita, he doesn't need to call me back, but if you could just tell him that for me, I'd appreciate it." She hung up the phone quickly with a deep breath.

Sydney stumbled into the kitchen to start the coffee that she had become so attached to, before calling Becky. Becky, of course, talked a mile a minute without seeming to be aware of the fact that Sydney had not said a word since hello. After Sydney politely fibbed and said that she wouldn't be needing any help until later that afternoon, she practically gulped her first cup of coffee down without so much as a breath. Becky was a doll, but Sydney wasn't quite ready for all of that energy right yet. They decided that 2 p.m. Becky would come over and start helping. Sydney told her that she wanted to get things separated and organized before packing, that way she could see what needed to be discarded, donated, or kept. Sydney knew that four hours wasn't enough time to do hardly anything, but it still allotted her a little breathing space.

Even with the restful night of sleep, her eyes still felt as if they had been rubbed with sandpaper and her body ached all over. After stretching, she decided on starting in her father's room first. After a couple of hours, she stood from her task at hand and rubbed her shoulders. The last couple of weeks she had been running on fumes, with little to eat and little sleep. Sydney felt emotional and knew that it, in large, was due to the fact that she lacked the physical strength and energy to ward off those harmful feelings of despair. Sydney ran her finger's through her hair and felt her eyes, once again, fill up.

Sydney very rarely gave into these emotions. Not because she was cold or unfeeling, but because she felt weak when she gave way to them. Had any other person had the life that Sydney had, they'd be both grateful and ironically, ready to collapse from the hurt and despair she had had to endure. Sydney remarkably had endured it all and even rose above it, with the tenacity of an alley cat. Her life wasn't easy, nor did she ever expect it to be so. Sydney's expectations were never very high, because of those *life's lessons*. This way, she was rarely disappointed.

As she sat back down and bowed her head, she sobbed with all of the emotions of pain, anger, despair, and the ugliest one of all, self loathing. After feeling she couldn't drop another tear, she wiped her face with the sleeve of her sweatshirt. Sydney felt paralyzed, stuck in this moment. She had been like this for months, long enough to give her the feeling that this is where she would stay.

THE EARLY *years*

CHAPTER *four*

It all began when Sydney was nine years old. Up until then, she had had the normal family life. Her parents were loving, caring, good, and hard working. There was laughter that had filled this old house, so many years ago, but something happened that muffled the laughter. The laughter lost its passion. It was more composed, unresponsive, and not quite as innocent as it once was. Looking out the window again, Sydney could remember that day that had changed the course of her life, as if it were yesterday.

Her mother hadn't been feeling very good and after waiting for the pain to go away and trying to remedy it herself, to no avail, she had finally given in to going to see the doctor. After sending Sydney off to school, her father drove her mother to her doctor's appointment. The doctor asked Sally the usual "doctor/patient" type questions, where she was feeling the pain, how often, etc. The doctor, after getting some answers from Sally, had some suspicions, but wouldn't voice them until he had the tests run and was sure. Sydney's mother, Sally, after answering all the questions that the doctor had thrown at her, had no idea that this could be something that couldn't be cured with some sort of remedy, so she didn't even bat an eye.

Upon leaving the doctor's office, he assured her that he would call her as soon as the results from the test's he took came back. They both walked out of his office, with Charles arm slung lazily around her shoulders. As the doctor watched them leave, he wondered how such a handsome, happy couple would deal with his suspicions, if they were found to be true. That was when he despised being a doctor. He had become one so that he could heal people and relieve the pain that they were in, not so that he could be the one to give them their death sentence, and sit there helplessly while he watched their faces crumple into tears and agony. He sighed deeply as he returned to finishing up some of his notes, so that he could attend to his next patient.

The following week, Sydney had just gotten home from school, with her face flushed from the walk home, and dropped her backpack on the kitchen table, yelling for her mom. "Mom, I'm home. What are we having for dinner?" She queried, as she ran up the stairs, taking them two at a time.

"I'm in the laundry room, honey. How was your day at school?" Her mother responded with a kiss on the cheek, while ignoring Sydney's question about dinner.

"Oh, it was fine, but my teacher gave us *a lot* of homework to do tonight. She can be so mean sometimes, just because of that stupid kid, Jeff! He wouldn't stop talking and goofing around, so she said that since she had to take so much of her time, trying to get him to listen, we'd have to do it on our time! Do you think that's fair, Mom? I don't and the whole class is pretty mad at him. No wonder he doesn't have any friends!"

"Well hon, I suppose your teacher is right. I know it seems unfair to get punished for someone else's behavior, but maybe in doing this, she's hoping to get some help from the class, since *she* can't seem to get him to behave. Maybe she's relying upon the class to make him feel so bad, that he'll not do it again," her mother replied, while snapping a towel before folding it.

"Listen, I'll be starting dinner pretty soon, your father called and said he probably will be home a little earlier tonight, so I thought I'd make him his favorite meal. Good 'ole Southern fried Chicken, mashed potatoes, corn, gravy, and some hot buttery biscuits, with some warm peach cobbler topped with vanilla ice cream, yum. How's that meet with your approval, Sydney, dear?"

Sydney grinned at her mother's last statement, for she had been complaining to her mother that she never made them good dinners anymore. It always was something quick and easy, since most of the time, lately, her father was working late at the shop and would just grab something from the diner down the street, that is, if he took the time to eat dinner at all. Sydney's grin was all the answer that her mother needed to know that, it did, indeed, meet with her approval.

Sally always thought that Sydney was just like her father in so many ways. Just this last year, Sydney started growing and growing and growing, that Sally feared she would never stop. Sydney was already even with her mother's height. As far as looks, Sydney and Sally were images of each other, but where Sally was petite and only five foot three inches, Sydney had inherited her father's height and bone structure. Sydney and her mother both had thick, curly, auburn hair and very light brown eyes that looked like gold topaz. Their skin was olive in complexion. While her father was a very handsome man, he had light brown hair, which had started to gray around the edges. His eyes were a deep ocean colored blue and a dimple right smack dab in the middle of his chin. They were a very attractive family, but they didn't seem to notice it, as they'd often get admiring stares from others.

Up to this point, they seemingly had a carefree life, no real ups or downs. There weren't any rollercoaster type events in their lives. Sydney was a good child and her parents loved each other. Some would say it was too perfect, that they were due for a monkey wrench to be thrown in, to unsettle their *perfect world* just a bit.

"Okay then, hon, you go get cleaned up and started on your homework, since you have so much of it. As soon as I finish folding the last of these towels, I'm going downstairs to get started on dinner."

The phone started ringing almost before Sally finished with her sentence. With a sigh at having to be interrupted before she finished the last of the towels, she answered it just in time to keep it from being picked up by the answering machine. Hearing her doctor's voice on the other end, made her glad the machine didn't pick up.

"Sure, I can be there tomorrow, first thing in the morning."

After a brief silence, Sally uttered a response, as she nervously ran her fingers through her hair as she often did when she was frustrated or worried. "Uh, no, I'll be coming alone. Charles has been overwhelmed with work at the shop and I don't want to ask him to take another day off on my account. Is there some reason that you needed him there?" Sydney's mother bluntly asked the doctor.

Obviously, the doctor wasn't going to tell her anything over the phone, so he only confirmed her appointment, once again, and told her he would speak with her then.

Sydney stood in the hallway, until her mother hung up, so that she could find out who it was. Sally didn't see her daughter standing there as she slowly set the phone back into the handset, with a concerned look on her face. As soon as she glimpsed Sydney, the concern was gone, as if Sydney had imagined it.

"Now young lady, I thought that I gave you some instructions to follow and why aren't you doing them?" her mother inquired, with her hands placed on her hips.

"I just thought maybe the phone would be for me. Who was that anyhow?" Sydney boldly questioned her.

"Oh, it was just my doctor wanting me to stop by his office tomorrow, to pick up the results of the tests that I had done last week. Now you scoot back on up into your room and get that homework started, so that you can enjoy dinner."

Sally smiled as she heard Sydney mumbling something about wishing she would never had told her mother about all of her homework, as she trudged to her room, as if she had leaden feet. As Sydney sat down at her small desk, she reached down to pull one of her books out of her backpack and threw it on her small desk by the window to get her homework over with. All of her concentration was directed by a story problem in math that she was trying to solve that she jumped when she realized her mother was standing quietly right behind her, just watching her. Again that uneasy feeling needled at her thoughts, when she jumped from being startled. "Mom, you about scared me half to death!"

"I didn't mean to, sweetie, I just didn't want to interrupt all of that concentration that you were exhibiting. But anyway, I wanted to ask you if you wouldn't mention the phone call from the doctor this afternoon to your father when he gets home. He's been working himself so hard lately. With this being the first night in quite some time that he has been able to come home early and relax, I really don't want him to think that he should take another day off, to go with me. It's really pointless; besides, he'll just worry."

Sydney may have only been nine years old, but she sensed something more, and remembering the look on her mother's face as she hung up the phone, knew that there was more to this than her mother was prepared to tell her.

"No, I won't say anything about it, mom, but what's the big deal anyhow? I mean, the doctor's not going to operate on you or anything tomorrow, is he?" Sydney responded with all the sarcasm she could get away with. Sydney was fishing for the questions she had wanted to ask earlier, but knew that she had better not push it too much. It was obvious to Sydney in how her mother's mood had changed from before the phone call and afterwards. Her mother, all of the sudden, seemed preoccupied and nervous, as if she were trying to hide something. Sydney didn't like this and after they had all eaten the dinner, she excused herself, even without touching dessert, and escaped into her room. She turned on her radio, with thoughts like thunder rolling through her head. Sydney uneasily sensed that something was wrong, but she didn't really realize how very much that "appointment" would change her life.

CHAPTER *five*

The next morning went as every other morning, as Sydney got ready for school, she could hear bits and pieces of her parents muffled conversation coming from the kitchen downstairs. As she grabbed her backpack and started down the stairs, she heard her father asking her mother if she still wanted to paint the extra bedroom upstairs, so that she could make it into a little office where she could do the bookwork for the shop. She had always done it from the kitchen table and would complain that it always looked cluttered and unorganized. Sydney's father owned the mechanic's shop in town and had a very good reputation for being honest and the best. People would come from a couple of town's over, just to have him work on their vehicles.

"If business keeps going the way it has, I'm going to have to find a larger place to put the shop and probably hire a couple of more guys to do some of the basic mechanic's work. That would lessen my burden and would free-up a lot of my time to focus on the specialty work that brings in the most money. Don't you agree, Sal? Plus, I think that it would keep you busy cooking these delicious dinners every night for me, because then, I'd be able to enjoy dinner every night with my gorgeous wife and daughter. Maybe, we could even throw around the possibility of taking some kind of *exotic vacation*," Charles said proudly, as he walked up behind his wife and moved her curly hair away from her neck, long enough to kiss her tenderly right beneath her lobe.

Sally felt the usual reaction to his kiss in that particular spot, as the goosebumps started to rise on her arms. "Still got it, don't I?!" Charles boasted, as he strutted back to the table.

Sally simply shook her head as she watched him act like a teenager over her shoulder. She turned back to the stove where she was turning the bacon over, as she felt a sad feeling creeping over her. She didn't have the nerve to turn around and face him, because he'd read her like a cheap two dollar novel. Her anxiety had increased with thoughts of the doctor and why he had to have her physically come in, rather than just tell her over the phone. Or for that matter, why *he* called her himself, rather than just have his receptionists do it, and the way he danced all around her questions yesterday also confirmed the fact that this was *not* going to be something minor. She was scared and fought the urge to turn to Charles and cling to him, so that he could give her the assurance that she needed. She wanted him to hold her and tell her that nothing bad was going to happen to her. But she wouldn't cave in to those feelings. Sally wanted to prolong the normalcy in their lives as long as possible, without disturbing anything in Charles,' Sydney's, or even her own life, until what was wrong with her was confirmed.

"You know, Charles, I think we *should* take a vacation. You've been working so hard these last couple of years that not only didn't you have time for a vacation, but you barely stop to even sleep! Maybe I'll run into town today and stop by that little Travel Bureau and pick up some brochures, then after dinner, we can all have some fun by picking out the one's we like. I know that Sydney would be just delighted, speaking of which, where is that little girl? Her breakfast is almost ready and I hope that she's not wearing that dreadful t-shirt again, that I told her not to wear to school anymore, because it's so ratty. She's just like you, Charles. Sydney doesn't care what she has on as long as she's comfortable. I imagine it's so that she can remain the tomboy that I doubt she'll ever grow out of," Sally complained, just before yelling for Sydney, who was sitting in front of the television, as usual, totally oblivious to everything around her.

Sydney was soon sitting in class, checking her homework, when Jeff arrived, plopping down at his desk which sat right next to hers. Sydney ignored him, as he started his usual teasing towards her, about being a "little miss goody-two-shoes." Sydney could feel the blood go to her face in embarrassment, as Jeff gloated from getting the expected reaction from her. Sydney's parents would be surprised to find that Sydney had only one good friend in school and that she was excruciatingly shy and uncomfortable with her classmates. Being an only child didn't help Sydney's dilemma, either. She had always been around adults in her young life and somehow lacked the ability to socialize with others her age. The kids in her class took this as a personal insult and thought that rather than her being scared, she was being stuck-up because her family had a little more wealth than most of her peers. Her looks at that time in her life were more of a detriment than an asset, because not realizing how pretty she was, the other girls would not let her inside their little cliques, because they were jealous. Sydney had grown quite used to all of this and had adapted by becoming a loner and trying to become invisible, to avert some of the hostility. But Jeff seemed almost as if he knew how hard she tried to disappear and he was determined not to let her. Sydney was pretty much a loner in school, except for her best friend Marci, who unfortunately wasn't in her classroom this year.

Her parents were unaware that Sydney was so shy in school, because her father was too busy working all the time and her mother didn't notice the lack of invites to birthday parties and such, because Sydney was far from shy at home and seemed like every other normal nine-year-old girl.

Even with Jeff's badgering today, Sydney couldn't quite erase the worry from her mind about her mother's appointment this morning. But this time she didn't have anyone to talk to, because she couldn't stop by her father's shop on the way home and talk to him about it, because her mother had asked her not to tell him. Otherwise, she would have gone there straight after school and talked with him about it, and as usual, he'd make her feel foolish and assure her that everything was just fine, as he normally did. He had always had such an easy way about him when it came to difficult matters. He'd always smooth everything out, no matter how big or small the problem was.

CHAPTER *six*

After everyone left the house, Sally went upstairs to take a shower to get ready for her appointment. As she stood underneath the steady pulse of hot water, she started to soap down. Sally felt that all too familiar, gnawing pain start to stretch through her body. The pain felt like tentacles, with white hot tips, that she had become so used to having. It would come and go, sometimes the pain was only a dull ache and other time's it would become so intense, that her very breath would be taken away. She kept telling herself that everything was going to be fine, after all, she was only 34 years old.

Sally fought the dread that kept trying to intrude upon her thoughts. After her shower, she threw on an old faded pair of blue jeans, a light sweater, and her sneakers. After Sally quickly took a once over in the mirror, she placed a clip in the back of her hair to pull it up. Looking at her reflection, Sally smiled to herself thinking that Sydney was starting to rub off on her attire. As she grabbed her purse, she started down the stairs, glancing into the kitchen that was still in a state of disarray, but after checking the clock one more time, realized that she had better leave, otherwise she would be late.

As she walked out the front door, Gretta next door gave

her a wave and a holler as she was tending to some plants filled with colorful flowers on her front porch. She gave her a wave back. She wished that she had had time to clean the kitchen up before leaving; she didn't feel like having to come back to it, but there was no time. She hopped into her jeep that her husband kept pleading with her to give up and get something more modern, but she loved it. Besides, she had no real need for an expensive vehicle, when the only time she used one was to run errands. She found she didn't have a problem finding a parking spot at the medical center, being so early in the day, as she wheeled into a parking spot close to the entrance. She checked her wristwatch as she entered the building, noting that she was only a few minutes late. The doctor *always* seemed to keep her waiting, so turn about was fair play, she thought to herself as she stepped onto the elevator and pushed the button for the floor she needed. As she approached the receptionist, she gave her name and was preparing to sit down with one of the dated magazines that were always provided on one of the tables. But as she started, the receptionist informed her, with a smile, that the doctor was ready to see her in his office.

"Uh, oh, okay," Sally uttered as she placed the magazine back down.

As she entered the office, the receptionist asked her if she'd care for any water or coffee.

"No thank you," Sally replied as her mouth suddenly became dry, feeling that she was going to start crying at any given moment, from the expression on the face of her doctor. As she felt her knees go weak underneath her, she settled into the plush chair in front of his desk. She looked at her fingers that were wrapped around the handles of her purse on her lap. Her palms were growing clammy as they often did from nerves, as she shivered involuntarily. After looking at his somber expression and searching his eye's for some hint that this impending news wouldn't be as serious as she had imagined and finding none, Sally took a deep breath and steeled herself for the results.

Surprising both herself and him, Sally spoke first, with a no nonsense approach. "By the look on your face, I am suspecting that this isn't going to be good news. Before I hear it, I came here alone today, because somehow I knew that this is going to be bad, *real bad*, judging by the look on your face." Sally took a deep breath, hesitating for a moment, hoping that the doctor would intervene and tell her no, that it wasn't serious at all. When she realized he wasn't going to, she swallowed and continued. "Whatever you tell me today without my family here, will give me time to let it sink in, before I can prepare them for the news. I'm hoping to delay this news for them, so that they don't have to have their day ruined, as I suspect mine is going to be. Okay, just give it to me straight. I don't want to hear the word's 'maybe, if, or possibly,' I only want the facts. Not some kind of empty pipe dream. I want to know if I'm going to die, then I want to know how much time I possibly have. I want to know what kind of time I'm looking at to where I'll be able to manage every day normal tasks on my own. I want to know what to expect, in regards to pain, consciousness, and basically being independent."

As the doctor listened to her, he watched her face. She was fighting to remain composed while she spoke bluntly to him. She almost sounded as if she wanted to yell at him at times. The saddest thing was so how very young she looked right now. Sally appeared to look almost as young a teenager and as fragile as one, until you heard the determination in her tone of voice. She was being as tough as she could muster and he knew that even though she held her composure on the surface, that just underneath there was a bomb that was coming close to being launched.

He spoke as straight forward and as unemotionally as he could. "Sally, I'm afraid that I'm going to have to confirm your greatest fears. You have cancer and I was hoping that it would still be in the first stages, but, unfortunately, it's metastasized far too much to go in and try to clean it out. It's terminal." The doctor took a moment to let his last word sink in. "Its spread all throughout your body. By experience with this kind of cancer, it moves rapidly. Unfortunately, it's also hard to predict, but I'm afraid that you don't have more than six months.

"I'm quite astonished, Sally, that you haven't had considerably more pain than you have. If I could honestly give you a better diagnosis or some hope to cling to, believe me, I would. Being your doctor, I shouldn't probably say this to you, for you could probably sue me for malpractice, but you asked for me to be up front, so be it. I could tell you to try all the treatments there are, for instance, radiation, chemo, etc., but at this point, it would only prolong the inevitable, with a less than satisfactory quality of life, but those options *are* available to you, if that's what you choose to do. Honestly, in my opinion, I don't think that's what you want. But to ask you right now how you're going to feel in a month or two is like asking pigs to fly. Those treatments that I mentioned would diminish your quality of life, regarding lucidity, strength, etc, and quite frankly, it would be a losing battle. I think that you would rather enjoy what 'good time' you have left, without feeling bad all of the time, to just feeling bad most of the time. When the pain from the cancer becomes too much for you to bear, then we can adjust for that, then. I understand why you didn't bring your husband, but I wish you would have brought *somebody* with you today. One of the reason's I request a companion for instances like this is because I never know how one will react, in fact, I don't believe even they, themselves, are sure about their reaction, when they are given this kind of news. The one's I think won't fall apart, do. The one's I think will, don't . . . and then again, at some point they all fall apart. I have long since quit trying to express my bitter sorrow and deep, deep regret, at having to give you this news. I will never, ever be comfortable or used to this part of my career as a doctor. I hope you understand, is all that I ask. I am, after all, only the messenger."

The doctor stood up and came around to the front of his desk, as he leaned his hip on the edge, he reached over and grabbed one of his cards with his numbers on it, office, home, and an emergency number. "If you have anything at all come up that you're not sure about, do not hesitate to call me at any of those numbers. I don't give everyone these cards, but the one's I do hand them out to, I expect for them to use it. Again, if you have anything you're wondering about, call."

Sally sat there for a moment to absorb all that she had heard, while neither smiling nor frowning; as she stood up, she felt as if the number one heavy weight boxer had just given her body a blow to the gut. She didn't trust her voice to speak, so as she stood and nodded at the doctor, she took the card from his hand. She turned and walked out of his office using all the strength she could find, to escape the smothering feeling that had surrounded her. She didn't look back once, as she passed the secretary's desk, she looked up at Sally with a sympathetic smile, knowing the cards that she had just been dealt. Sally had an unnatural urge to slap that sympathetic smile right off of that receptionist, but as irrational a feeling as that was, that was the anger that Sally felt building inside of her.

After watching her leave his office, the doctor knew that her tears would come, but how many would follow after, he wondered. Why did it seem it always the one's that had so much life left and so much to live for, seemed to be the one's picked unfairly, before they were ripe. He dealt with so many people, some of them abusing their bodies, some of them abusing others, some of them old and hateful, and they never seemed to have to endure this kind of trauma. He shook his head, knowing that he would never understand it in his lifetime.

After reaching the front entrance way of the medical center, Sally fought the urge to run as fast as she could and as far away from this awful place as she could. Sally was all the while hoping upon hope, that she would wake up and realize that this was just some silly nightmare and that everything was fine. She knew that it was unrealistic to blame any of them, after all, didn't the doctor himself predict this feeling, "only the messenger" he said. But Sally didn't run, nor did she even walk quickly. She kept her head up and did all the normal, usual things that she would do on any given day. For instance, on her way out, out of habit, she held the door for an older gentleman with a walker, as he complained to her about getting old.

"Sorry, that's obviously something that I'll never have to worry about, sir," Sally replied bitterly. When the man registered what she had just said, he turned around and wanted to apologize, but she was already through the entryway. He didn't even get to tell her thank you for holding the door for him. As he looked down at his old worn brown speckled hands on his walker, he silently gave thanks and vowed not to complain about having to use a walker, but to rejoice at the fact that he was still able to.

On the way to her jeep, the words "six months" and "only the messenger" kept playing over and over in her mind till she felt her head would explode. She had anticipated something bad, would at this point had been eager to have only a breast removed, but not this! Nothing this absolute! He couldn't even give her the smallest possible glimmer of hope!

Sally thought to herself, "*I can accept the dying part, but the time that has been imposed is so unfair!*" As she approached the jeep, she wondered how she could possibly leave this world with so little preparation time. As that thought occurred to Sally, it quickly turned into the most ridiculous a thought she could have. Sally smiled grimly, *"No,"* she thought to herself, *"there is never a perfect time to die."* Sally's hands were trembling as she tried to place the key into the door to unlock it. After a few times, Sally took a deep breath and finally managed to successfully open it. As she climbed into the driver's seat, she started thinking about when or how she would tell Charles and Sydney.

Today is only Wednesday, Sally thought, *I should probably wait until it's not a school night. I should at least wait until the weekend.* Sally started laughing to herself, *yeah, that's probably a good idea, wait until the weekend, so that you can totally destroy any relaxation or fun that either one of them were planning on. Let's give them two whole days with nothing to do, but deal with my dilemma.*

Sally drove without even noticing anything on her way home but her thoughts. It was as if she was on auto-pilot and her mind was just a whirlwind of this news, playing it over and over and over. Upon arriving home, Sally felt as if she had been gone for days, instead of only a couple of hours. As she dropped her purse in the foyer on the table that everyone had seemed to have adopted for keys, sunglasses, back-packs, and purses. On some occasions, even a stray jacket that seemed to be too tired to make it to the closet, which had to be walked passed first, in order to reach the table. *Oh, but then, of course, you had to actually open the closet door and either reach for a hanger or just hook it on one of the many unused hooks that were provided for them.* Such a small, insignificant, daily occurrence that suddenly lost all importance to Sally and that she regretted wasting so much time nagging and whining to Sydney about it. Time lost. How many other things had she given such significance to that were really so minor and trivial; she didn't want to even think about such a needless waste of time that will never again be retrieved.

As she remembered how she had left the kitchen in such a chaotic mess, Sally even wondered if she should waste time on it. Now she had to laugh at herself, because that was just finding a reason to be downright lazy and an easy excuse to get out of cleaning it. After all, whether the kitchen was left dirty or clean, was of no incidence to her, after all, she had already received her death sentence and what else did she have planned for this morning and afternoon? Was she going to sit on the couch for six months and just wait for *Father Time*, that is, if he even waited that long! Better yet, maybe she should run up to the local mart and purchase some champagne, so that she could get just as drunk as she pleased. After all, abusing alcohol or drugs wasn't going to harm her at this point. All her life she had spent being so careful, eating right, watching her weight, getting enough exercise that she did with an aversion each and every morning, first thing. She started thinking about all the options that she had right now, *gee,* Sally thought, *I could go out and commit armed robbery or murder someone and they can't give me any more than six whole months for it.* Sally started laughing hysterically at her last thought and if at all possible, crying at the exact same time.

The sobs started as a small trickle at first and developed into a raging river as if someone had opened the dam and with all the pressure, couldn't shut it back up. As she slumped into one of the kitchen chairs, it seemed as if every emotion Sally tried so hard to keep in check all chose to surface at once. The sobs of agony erupted from her innermost core and bellowed out with a chilling sound. A rage with such force enveloped Sally and she tore the calendar off of the kitchen wall and ripped out each month that she had left, after seeing the one that she wouldn't be in existence for, she screamed and cried and with one fell swoop used her arm to slide everything on the kitchen table onto the floor, crashing and breaking into small slivers of what was once something whole! Oh wonderful, now self pity came marching in with gusto. Sally thought about Sydney, she would never see her daughter grow from a child into adulthood. *Who will my little girl talk to, go shopping with, nag at her about cleaning her room, doing her homework. And what about Charles, how will he take this, will he find someone to take my place, will he miss me, will he actually cry for once?*

Again, an overwhelming sadness took hold of Sally, mixed with pain and grief, again starting pitifully, then gaining momentum and finally rising into a crescendo; Sally was crying so uncontrollably that she couldn't even catch her breath. Sally hadn't shut the front door when she came home. As Sally heard something speak that wasn't coming from her, she looked up and found Gretta standing at the screen door, already having it half-way open, without any fear or unsureness.

CHAPTER *seven*

Gretta was their neighbor, actually, Sally and Charles had often referred to Gretta as their own little private angel. They were blessed by being her neighbor; she had become part of their family. She and Sally had become fast friends. They both kept each other company throughout the day, traded recipes, talked about raising children, dealing with husbands, and most of all, divulged their deepest and darkest secrets to each other without the fear of exposure.

Gretta was in her early sixties, but was much younger than that in her personality. She had plenty of experience about life and the wisdom to share with it, but she never behaved like some old *codger*. Her humor was notorious around town, her clothes were always of the latest fashion, her honesty in telling others what she thought could sometimes be wounding, but she was always forgiven. She was five feet five inches tall and had a figure that even younger women vied for, but she remained a widow, which dismayed many a gentleman caller.

Sally had been raised by her grandparents, never knowing her own parents. Her grandparents had died within one year of each other before Sydney was ever born. Charles' parents were both killed in a head on collision when he was 17 years old. So

Gretta had become the surrogate parent that they both needed in their lives.

For Sally, growing up with her grandparents was sometimes difficult for her in her young years. Having a young child, energetic, youthful, full of life, was not how her grandparents had anticipated sliding into their *golden years*. All Sally knew about her mother was that she ran away, leaving her daughter behind. Sally had learned very early never to ask about her. When she did, she received nothing, but a silent cold stare. Her grandparents brought her up in a strict religious household. They attended church, each and every Sunday, fasted for communion, and clutched their Bible's with self-righteousness. Sally was continually disappointing them, while being punished with words of hell and damnation. Their household was filled with silence, no laughter, no joy, no love, just a mere existence.

Charles' parents went to the other side of the coin. They were fun, very social, loved Charles, loved each other. His parents died one night after leaving an anniversary party of one of the couples that they socialized with often. Charles had been devastated by the news. Since he was already 17 years old and only had one year left of school to get through, he opted out of going to live with one of his distant relatives. He went to work right away, working full shifts, while at the same time trying to get through his last year of school that it didn't leave him time for anything else.

After a friend had repeatedly hounded him into going to a party, he finally agreed. That's where he met Sally. She wasn't supposed to be there, in fact, she had to sneak out of her bedroom window. That first night, they had talked late into the night. Charles had independence, where Sally had none, which made it increasingly difficult for the both of them to continue with their relationship. By the time Sally had reached her senior year, Charles had a full time job, with his own place to live. Sally could barely stand to wait until she graduated, but Charles thought it would be best. As soon as she did, Charles married Sally quietly, with only a few friends at the courthouse.

So when Gretta entered into their lives, she was a breath of fresh air. Sally found that God wasn't the same to Gretta as to what her grandparents had always taught her about Him. They made her think that God was this being that was always waiting to punish you for your wrong doings. She always felt as if He were sitting on the edge of His seat, waiting for her to mess up again, till she found that she didn't like Him very much. Gretta changed that for Sally, she showed her a new relationship with God. Gretta exuded His love and kindness through her smiles, cheerfulness, and found beauty in everyone and everything that she came into contact with.

Gretta had been widowed since she was only 39 years old, left alone to finish raising, not one, not two, but three highly active boys on her own. All the while, never missing a beat and doing a superb job of it to boot. She was a tough opinionated lady, but never lacked compassion for other's weaknesses. She loved Sydney from the day that Sally informed her that she was pregnant. She was there with Charles, when Sydney came into this world, and felt very honored at being included in such an intimate time.

She was the one that they would call, when they needed a night out alone together. Sydney, at times, would often go over to Gretta's house and just hang out with her, rather than hang out at home. Gretta always kept Sydney rapt with attention, when she'd tell her stories of the bible or when she was younger. Gretta seemed to be able to do anything and everything, and quite frankly, did. But the one thing that she loved more than anything else in this world was her flowers and her vegetable garden. Gretta passed over any man that would try to romance her to the altar, but yet, they never seemed to stop trying. Each and every one of them somehow felt that he would *be the one.* In the end, the only thing that they had to remember Gretta by was their broken hearts.

Charles told Sally that the reason Gretta attracted so many of them, was because of the challenge she posed and her vivacity for life. Gretta had confided to Sally one day, while talking about a particularly nice gentleman that Gretta actually even considered holding onto longer than the rest, that no one could ever receive the love that she had for her husband, John, who passed away much too early in life. Gretta was never idealizing John. Actually, she said that he was one of the *most* imperfect men she's ever come into contact with.

Sally was amazed that she and John had even stayed married after Gretta would tell her of some of the escapades he would pull or of the several arguments that they had. Gretta's motto is stick it out; that's the only way you'll learn each other and grow together. Gretta always complained about how people gave up so quickly now-a-days. If half of them listened to her, they'd realize how right she was. She said that after a little trouble that caused the relationship to become a little worn, they would leave. She would say, "Now that's just down right lazy! Do they think they're *ever* going to find someone who doesn't have *some kind of quirk,* or find someone in which they'll never have any *glitches*! How absurd and just plain ignorant!

"You know, Sally, I feel very very blessed that I had the honor of spending my life with a man that had given me so much in so little time. I am very lucky to be one of the few people in this world that can honestly know that they were given a great gift. For a very select few, there is a deep, steady, and unconditional love like that. I think that you and Charles have that kind of love, but the only way to be sure sometimes, ironically, is something that test's that love. It's quite easy to love someone, but to *be in love* is a whole entirely different matter. When things are good, it's never hard to maintain, but when they start to fall apart, that's the true test. Will that love still hold, or will it crumble as quick as however big the problem is? Sadly, it's usually the latter of the two." Sally remembered those words as clear as if she had just said them. She had told her that when Charles and she were going through their very first *big quake* in their marriage.

CHAPTER *eight*

So as Gretta hurried inside the house towards Sally, she knew something dreadful had happened. "Sally, what's happened?" As she looked around at the mess, thinking maybe someone had broken into the house.

Sally hiccupped as she tried to talk. "Gretta! Oh Gretta! I have to tell someone and I don't know how to tell even you!" Sally cried as she wiped her eyes and blew her nose, with all of the broken glass in shreds all over the kitchen floor and the calendar ripped and crumpled laying half on the chair and the other half almost reaching the floor.

Sally tried to gain her composure back, by straightening in her chair, forgetting all the glass and the mess, looking as if there had been a bomb or an earthquake recently. "Remember a long time ago, when I mentioned to you that I was feeling bad all of the time? Well, I finally went to see the doctor, as it turns out, I have *the big C*, I have cancer in the worst degree. It has spread its ugly arms throughout my body and nothing can be done to stop it. I won't live for more than six months, tops, probably less! I feel *so cheated*! I'm only 34 years old! My daughter is too young to be without her mother!

"Oh my God, oh God, not yet, please don't make me go

yet!" Sally was bent over with her arms hugging her middle rocking back and forth. "I'm so angry! Why didn't I go to the doctor sooner? It's my own fault! I should have seen the doctor a long time ago! But no, instead I wait and wait till I have absolutely *no choice at all to make,* and am given the final notice! Gretta, people *always* go before the time that the doctor tells them. I don't know what to do. When is a good time to inform my family that I'm going to be leaving them and not returning? Shall I just act like normal? Shall I tell them now, or wait until the pain *really* sets in? There will never be a good time. Why couldn't I just die in an auto crash, or fire? Why does the All Mighty God in heaven find it necessary to give me notice of my death and impose it in such a short time period? God, are you listening, can you hear me? Death row inmates have more time than I do! I've led a good life, I've never harmed anyone, I've always been kind, and I've always been honest, so can someone please tell me why, please, please tell me why!"

Gretta let Sally express her pain and anger and didn't intervene, for she understood all that Sally was feeling, not only did she feel that way when her beloved John fell ill, but she was feeling that way at this very moment. As Gretta bent down and pulled Sally's head onto her shoulder, she looked up and silently cursed God for making her feel this pain again and for taking another beautiful human being out of her life. Gretta softly whispered to Sally that everything would be fine and having said that, knew that those words sounded so shallow and hollow to her.

Gretta pulled away from Sally and lifted her face to hers by gently placing her finger underneath her chin. "Sally, I want you to look at me for a moment. I don't blame you one bit for having the feelings that you're having, but, and it's a *big but,* you cannot tell your family until you can do so with strength and grace. Right now, it's very fresh, it's scary, it's unfair, and there is nothing *anyone but God* can do to change this. But you have to deal with this yourself before you can be strong enough to tell them. Now listen, I'm going to make you a nice cup of hot tea while you let the world go, for just this moment, don't worry about your family, try if you can, to think about nothing at all. While you drink the tea, I'll go upstairs and start a nice warm bubble bath for you just to sit and soak in for a while. Trust me, it *will* relax you and that's all you need to worry about right now. I'll clean the kitchen up and make some nice hot fresh bread. But before all of that, I want you to lie down and take a nice nap after your bath, you need to rest," Gretta said to Sally kindly, looking at her tear streaked face.

Sally's energy seemed to dissipate all at once. She was thankful that Gretta appeared when she did, still being her own private Angel from Heaven. Even having this one person to talk with seemed to unload all the weight from Sally's body. Just letting go and letting someone else take over for a while was a great amount of burden taken off of her shoulders for that moment. Sally just nodded to Gretta with a grateful look.

Gretta rose and busied herself with putting the dirty dishes into some hot soapy water as she waited for the teapot to hiss at her. As she looked over her shoulder at Sally, she could see that she was deep in thought, but no longer crying. Gretta wished the sentence that had been given to Sally had instead been imposed on herself. But nothing in life ever seemed to go the way Gretta thought that it should. The memories of her husband's death started to come alive all over again, as if it only happened yesterday. She had been the one who was angry, she was the one that needed the consoling, and she was the one who wanted an explanation from God. She remembered after finding out the news, her husband's behavior. He told her of what the doctor said, as if he were telling her what the weather was going to be that day. Gretta's husband, John, had always been a spiritual man and always believed that God had his reasons for everything, whether good or bad. She couldn't remember him ever questioning God. He never doubted God's way.

After John informed her of this news, she railed at God. Gretta, at times, found it hard to get out of bed in the morning, with John feeding the children breakfast and sending them off to school, all the while whistling away, as if he were the happiest man on earth. Finally, one morning, after becoming increasingly irritated by this behavior, Gretta dragged herself out of bed and stomped down the stairs carrying her anger. She expressed her fury to him by asking him irritably how he could just be so nonchalant about it all and told him as much.

"Ah, Gretta my darling, what has put you in such a foul mood? You say you are annoyed at my cheerfulness? Well then, why don't you tell me how I should behave? Will it make you feel any better if I just curl up into a little ball and await my death? Or do you want me to enjoy my family for the time that *I do* have left? Do you want me to act miserable and feel sorry for myself? Well, I won't and can't. I'm not very sorry at all, to be honest, I feel a great peace from within that our God has chosen to take me this time into his arms. Of course, my family is very important to me and I don't want to leave any of you. But you really must stop feeling sorry, not for me, but for yourself! You are being selfish, because even though your sadness is partly for me, it's even more so for yourself. Look upon this as a blessing, my dear. We have loved deeply and unconditionally. Even one year of the love that we've had to share with each other is so much more than others who have spent their whole entire lives seeking. You need to be strong, for yourself, then for our children. You certainly don't want them to learn to collapse every time something doesn't go quite right in their lives, do you? Strength is the key, my dear; every time you become weak, you are inviting all the bad things to come into your life, self pity, failure, unhappiness, and anger. You will only become bitter from it, rather than grow and learn. Death to me is not the end, but the beginning of a beautiful future. Someday, we'll be together again, but in the meantime, do something powerful with your life and make a difference in just *one* person's life, that's what I expect from you. Don't ever let me watch you perched on the sidelines and giving up on life, that's not the Gretta I married, nor the person I want to remember. I am sorry if you feel insulted by what I have said to you this morning, but *I love you deeply and I need you by my side*, until my day is here. Every moment has become ever more precious for me I cherish it so much more. I wish that I always had, but again, I have learned how important some things really are and have learned to dismiss the things that aren't. Now my sweet, I want you to go and get dressed. I want to take you somewhere special today, okay?" John looked to Gretta expectantly, as if waiting for her to argue or say no.

Gretta stood there, stunned and embarrassed for her behavior. She had never looked at it that way and realized that he was right. She had wasted a good week of his time, using all of her own energy to wallow in her own self pity, rather than treasure the moments that they had left together. Gretta looked to him now with more love than she thought she was capable of, and went into his arms.

John looked down to her and deeply into her eyes and in them she saw the love he, in turn, had for her, as his eyes started to shine with tears waiting to drop. "Gretta, don't think for one single moment of the day that I would have chosen to leave you or my boys right now had I been given that option, but since I have no choice, I find peace in trusting in God's will. I want our family to have happy memories of the end of my life, rather than sadness. Please don't mourn me before

I am even gone. You'll have more than enough time for that after I am. Now you scoot, beautiful, before I have to dress you myself!" John lightly patted her on the bottom and turned her in the direction of the stairway gently with a soft nudge.

She glanced at him before going up; he had already turned away and started whistling again. As she started up the stairs, she wondered how in the world she would live without him. He let her borrow some of his strength, by letting her lean on him when she needed to; he calmed her, when her emotions had become uncontrollable and she was unable to think straight; he showed her so many new avenues, by teaching her so many things about life; he laughed with her, and oh how she would miss those nights when they stayed up far too late talking and sharing their thoughts with each other like teenagers. He was a very wise man with a very old soul. He had such an understanding about life and the people around him, that she sometimes found it quite amazing.

After readying herself for his "someplace special" adventure, she came downstairs to find he had filled a picnic basket full of goodies and a nice bottle of sparkling grape juice, with some fresh cut flowers from her garden, with a great big soft looking blanket laying beside the basket.

After arriving to his destination, she realized that he must have had to drive around for hours to find the most beautiful place she'd ever seen to have their picnic. It was perfect. The wild flowers seemed to be endless, for as far as her eyes could see they were surrounded by them, and in the midst of all these beautiful colors, stood one lonesome big old tree that had green plush grass surrounding it. It almost seemed as if this area had been expecting them. The only sounds she could hear were some birds chirping and insects buzzing around. It was magical and almost impossible to believe that it was so untouched and pure. John couldn't have special ordered a more beautiful day, nor a more peaceful spot.

After he got everything situated for them under the tree, he straddled her as she sat in between his legs and leaned her back against him, while they talked and talked, giggled and laughed about everything; it was almost as if they were getting to know one another all over again. Even before finding out about his illness, they had drifted away from spending time like this together. *He was so right,* Gretta thought to herself as she fed him another piece of cheese on a cracker, *even as ugly as death can seem, it really does wake you up and changes your priorities as to the truly important things in life and it's time like this,* Gretta thought. They spent the whole entire day there. When their bellies had become full from nibbling on all of the delicious snacks that John had packed, Gretta assumed that they would be leaving for home again.

"I'll carry these things to the car, while you relax for a while, John," Gretta said when he seemed to become a little restless sitting there. She was afraid that he was starting to be in pain.

John grabbed her as she started to get up and pulled her back down. "Oh no you don't, you're not taking one dog gone thing to that car, in fact, I want you just to pretend that that car isn't even here. That we are stranded, no running water, no television, no VCRs, no radios, no car horns, not one single noise is here except the ones that are *supposed* to be here. I am in no hurry to leave, the boys aren't at home, and there is not one thing urgent enough to interrupt my time here. As far as I'm concerned, I have everything I want or need, right here, right now, with the exception of my boys, and am very very content at the moment. What about you, are you getting restless?"

"I just thought that it was you who was getting restless, or that you were in pain," Gretta said, mad at herself for bringing up his ugly disease and reminding not only herself, but John too. She looked at his cancer as she would an uninvited or unwanted intruder into her home.

"Now you know that I would tell you if I was in a lot of pain, but I'm not, so therefore we stay put right here, okay?"

"John, I wish that we never had to leave this place, it's magical. I feel as I look out across the valley at all the beauty here; that it's not real. I cannot believe that no one has touched it and started building houses, or factories."

"I betcha I can tell you why? No one can, and *do* you know why they can't, because they'd have to get permission from me, *the property owner*." He watched her face slowly conceive what he just told her, as she slowly turned her face towards him, with her mouth dropped open.

"What on earth are you talking about John? I would know if you bought this property, for it would cost a fortune for all of this beauty!"

"How come you would know? I bought this property here just before we were married, Gretta. I am sorry that this is the first time that I've brought you here, but let me explain. Just before we were married, you had always talked about a spot like this that you wanted some day, so that you could have room for your dogs to run as far as they wanted to and so that you and I could take nice long leisurely walks together, without having to run into another human. You probably don't remember telling me that one evening, but I'll never forget it, Gretta. Your eyes glistened and your face shone with happiness at just the mere thought of it. Even though I had already asked you for your hand in marriage and you had agreed, that moment sealed it forever in my heart. That's when I purchased this piece of property. The reason that I have never taken you here, is not because I didn't want you to know, but because I wanted to give it to you as a surprise on our twenty-fifth wedding anniversary. I know what you're thinking, that it sounds nuts to buy a present for someone so many years before giving it to them, and it was. I obviously can be quite the romantic or watched too many movies, either way, when I had came across it, I fell in love with it and knew that I would be making a mistake if I didn't buy it. Obviously, at that young age, I didn't anticipate the fact that either one of us might die before our twenty-fifth anniversary, but the one thing that I was absolutely sure of, was that we would spend the rest of our lives with one another. I've never for even one single split second wavered in confidence about that fact. I hope that you're not hurt that I have kept this from you. I know that I'm certainly just more than a little irritated at myself for that right now! I feel rather the fool. I have always mocked other's who stowed their precious china, never taking it out to be enjoyed and used for their pleasure. Or the cars that were never driven, sitting with a cover over them, never taking them out for a joy ride, because they were afraid that they might get a ding in their sides.

"Here I sit on a beautiful peace of property, holding it for that one *big moment* and that moment has vanished, along with all the times that we could have brought the boys out here to run and play. Gretta, it's not just the property that I am speaking of, it's everything. I've left so many words unspoken, too many hugs not given, and so much love not shared and why? Guess I've been always waiting for that one *big moment*, well it's finally arrived, except I don't have quite enough time now."

"Oh my God, John, please don't be disappointed! I'm glad that you did keep it from me. Do you have any idea how *beautiful that is to me*? How unbelievably romantic that is? Or how very special, loved, and blessed you have made me feel? I have never watched a movie, read a book, or listened to a song that had anything even remotely more romantic than that. I want to tell the whole wide world of this, but I really don't think that one person would believe that someone could be so romantic!"

"Well, I have already had the paperwork taken care of and a little nest egg tucked away for the taxes you'll have to pay on this. There should be enough left over that you can build that small, and I do mean *small*, home out in the middle of nowhere just like you've always dreamed of having. As for the dogs, well, you are on your own!" John stood up, putting his hand out, "Come on, give me your hand and go for a walk with me, gorgeous."

"John, are you sure you're up to it?"

"Ssshhh, I want to hold your hand and have neither one of us say a word and just completely absorb all the beauty and fresh air surrounding us, while feeling the warmth of each other's hands."

After they both approached the blanket, still holding one another's hands, after their walk, Gretta felt as if the time they spent without speaking and enjoying the views, touched her heart more than any words of love uttered to her ever have.

"I'm just a little winded from that walk, but I enjoyed it. How about we both lie down on the blanket and have just a short nap, I'm not ready to leave yet, are you?"

"Not in the least. I'm so relieved that you want to stay, because this day has been *the* most beautiful day that I do believe that I've ever had in my whole entire life, or *will have!*"

Gretta nestled her head on his arm as they both succumbed to sleep, drifting off in each other's arms, as if they had not a worry or care in the world.

She awoke to John kissing her on the cheek. As it took a moment for her to gather her surroundings, she realized that the sun had fallen quite a bit in the sky.

"Would you just look at that sunset? You know, Gretta, all these years I thought that I appreciated things like the sunsets, the sound of the rain hitting the window pane, the laughter of children, the bird's talking to each other. I don't know I could go on and on about so many things, but one way of looking at my situation positively, is that it's made me see things that I often let go unnoticed, because I have taken so much for granted. It's made my listening better I hear words filled with love and kindness more than I did before. It's made my sense of smell much more sensitive to things such as a freshly mowed lawn, flowers, or just plain good clean air, but mostly, my most favorite smell is when you're baking a nice homemade loaf of bread. For the most part, I don't have many regrets, the biggest one, is having to leave my family, but I do regret having not paid attention to all of these things I have mentioned. People take so many things for granted, like the sunsets, so what if they miss one they'll always be another sunset tomorrow. But the one thing I have found to be true, is that 'tomorrow is promised to no one.' The day I listened to the doctor giving me my prognosis has changed every single moment of our lives. It amazes me how quickly that can happen. Gretta, I know that you think that I'm fine with all of this, but to be honest with you, I have many, many emotions running through me constantly. There is going to come a time with my illness, that you will need every ounce of strength and fortitude to let me lean on you for a bit. And you're the toughest person I know to take on that job, thank God!" As he played like he was a boxer.

"You had better believe it, so you had better mind your P's and your Q's! After all, I don't mind it, that you have become totally dependent on me, it makes me feel so *in charge*!" Gretta jokingly told him.

"I hate to say this, smarty pants, but I think you always have been.

"We had better call it a day, my dear, the sun has set and before long the mosquitoes will have us for dinner and trust me, that is one thing that I haven't ever let go unnoticed, nor wish to experience anymore," John said as he slapped one on his arm.

John passed away much sooner than expected for any of them. It was almost as if he had waited for her to gather up her strength. She was thankful that he didn't have to endure a lot of pain. While she sat with him in his last hours, he regained consciousness just long enough to give her a smile and whisper that he would be waiting for her. After his last breath, she laid her head upon his chest and finally realized that he was gone and wouldn't be coming back. She bowed her head to pray, something that she seemed to be doing more and more every day. She prayed for guidance, strength, and her children. At the very end, it was almost as if she were talking to one of her children rather than God, but with her tear streaked face, she raised her eyes to the heavens and didn't ask, but ordered, "*Now you had better take very good care of my husband, otherwise you will be answering to me!*"

CHAPTER *nine*

As Gretta was sweeping the mess up in Sally's kitchen, she snickered to herself, wondering if her dear Lord found that amusing. She had to believe that he and John got a big kick out of that one. She could just see John sitting next to God and saying, "*Yep, that's my girl! Sorry 'bout that one, Jesus, but sometimes she forgets her size and who she's talking to. Tough as steel, she is . . .*"

Gretta never let go of John's words, nor did she ever once push God out of her life. She went through those first few weeks of adjustments as best she could. There were times when she wanted to curl up into a little ball and hide her head, hoping upon hope that some sort of "Super Hero" would take over, so that she didn't have to "deal" with anything anymore. There were times when she wanted to let go of the anger she often felt welling up inside, but the worst feeling in the world was the times that she became lonely and missed John so much that she thought she might die from the pain and sadness. Somehow Gretta managed, the boy's managed, and by all of them working together and leaning on each other, they began to smile and laugh as a family once again. The only difference was that their circle was just slightly smaller.

After taking one last look to make sure that she had gotten the kitchen back to order, she listened for any movements upstairs and set Sally's oven on preheat. She quickly went back to her house next door and grabbed the dough that she had made yesterday, intending to bake it today anyway. She decided that she'd just do it over there. She grabbed her shears out of the kitchen drawer and grabbed one of the grocery bags that she always saved and had far too many of them, but always thought that she could use them for this or that, but never had. She went out back to her garden and picked a couple of the biggest, juiciest tomatoes that she could find, putting them in the sack, she then went and snipped some roses off of her rose bush.

That rose bush was her pride and joy, when she first purchased this "little stick" (as John liked to call it), everyone told her that it wasn't going to grow. That only made her more determined to prove all of them wrong and it became a standing joke between John and her, especially in the beginning, when she almost had decided to give up. She had spent day after day giving it tender loving care, and it stubbornly refused to submit. Then after deciding she was going to yank it out and give up, she put on her weeding gloves and grabbed the shovel out of the shed, all the while not being the least bit happy about being proven wrong. Gretta started doing her usual muttering, and as she approached her rose bush, she couldn't believe her eyes. There it was, this lone little bud. She was so excited she could hardly wait until John came home from work. Her boys didn't give a hoot about her garden, flowers, or even fresh homemade bread. In fact, they were so disinterested in any of this, that to this day, she wasn't sure whether they even knew that their vegetables didn't come from the produce department at the store. *What difference does it make anyhow, she thought, the*

one thing that they did know, was that they ate well, and so did she
by the amounts of food that they went through every week!

After she clipped enough to fill a vase, she grabbed the rest
of the items and zipped right back next door. She quietly put
the dough into the oven, placed the tomatoes by the sink waiting to be washed, and found a vase underneath Sally's sink to
place the roses in. She set them in the middle of her table and
sat down and just admired her handiwork. Gretta had so many
wonderful memories that she was sure that they were what had
sustained her for all of these years alone.

As Gretta washed and started slicing her fat, juicy ruby red
tomatoes into big thick slices, she took a quick look to check
on her bread. She grabbed herself a cup of the tea that she had
made for Sally and sat back down at the table. Gretta could
remember when Sally and Charles bought this house. She was
out in her garden working and as she put the back of her hand
up to wipe the sweat off of her forehead, she actually heard
them before seeing them. As she watched this young happy
couple walk out to the backyard to look at it, she remembered
Sally's enormous smile as she looked back to Charles. It was
obvious to anyone watching her that she loved this home, but
even though Gretta could hear their voices, she couldn't make
out any words. After she realized that she was staring at them,
with a bit of envy, she went back to her gardening, thankful
that they didn't spot her staring as she had. She didn't want
anything, like having a nosy neighbor, diminish any of the
excitement that they were having. She had become so involved
in her gardening, that she had forgotten all about them and
was startled, when out of the corner of her eye, she spotted a
woman's foot. They almost seemed to be standing on top of her,
as Gretta let out a gasp.

"I'm so sorry I didn't mean to scare you." Sally's young
innocent face had gone red.

"I'm the one that should feel foolish. I forget that there is a world around me sometimes, when I'm out here," Gretta explained as she leaned her hand on one knee to stand up.

"Um, my a well, my husband and I were, um, looking at the house next to you that's for sale and I noticed how large your garden is. It must be very time consuming and by judging by how beautiful it is, you must have spent an enormous amount of time in it. I've never been very good with stuff like this, but I admire the people who are."

"Thank you, but it's really rather easy; the hardest part is having the discipline to weed it and all of the other little tedious things that go along with it. I've always compared having a garden to exercising every day. Most of us don't feel like doing it, but afterwards, we're always glad that we did. Please forgive me, my name is Gretta, and yours?" as Gretta peeled her glove off to shake Sally's hand.

Sally's husband was walking towards them after talking with what was probably the realtor showing them the home. "My name is Sally and this is my husband, Charles."

They spent a little time making small polite conversation and soon said their goodbyes. They seemed to be pretty nice, but Gretta had kind of gotten used to not having any neighbors on that side of her and even enjoyed it. She didn't know why that home had stood vacant for so long, but they seemed to have just adored it, so it didn't matter now. They were so young, and still were, but then they didn't seem old enough to be married, let alone purchasing a home. Gretta and Sally ended up hitting it off right from the start. For Gretta and Charles, the friendship took longer, the reason being he was hardly ever home, with the exception of evenings. Back then, Charles was a struggling business owner. As Gretta thought back to those earlier years, she realized how hard he worked to succeed at that business and how proud he was whenever asked about it.

Gretta bowed her head while she sat at the kitchen table, after admiring her beautiful roses, and prayed for God to give her the strength and guidance that Sally would need. Gretta felt some kind of intuitive feeling at stopping over here at the instant that she did. Gretta didn't believe in coincidences; she felt almost as if she had been taken by an invisible hand, leading her here. She was supposed to be here for Sally and suddenly felt insecure and anxious that she might possibly fail. Gretta frowned as she thought about how Sally blamed herself for not knowing to go to the doctor sooner. When as ridiculous as it was, it was an enormous guilt to carry and far too heavy. Sally had kept saying that if she were to do this or if she would have done that that this wouldn't have happened to her. Gretta was of the belief that each one of us, no matter what we do, has a designated day and time of death that was already written on the day of our conception. So therefore, Gretta felt it was total nonsense for Sally to have those feelings of guilt, for some things are not in our control. For everything, bad or good in our life, there is a reason for it, as she remembered John's words. Gretta only wished it weren't so hard to find the reason, but sometimes we never see it for what it is in the first place. We find ourselves looking for something obvious, rather than realizing it was there all the time and we just didn't notice, because we're always expecting something so much more complex.

Gretta had been very blessed with her boys. They were all grown and had their own lives. They had become such strong, mature, and kind men that she was astonished at times, that these were really her sons. Gretta enjoyed joking with others about how it was all because of her. She knew that even though they didn't get to spend a large part of their lives with their father, they did get to spend a significant part of it with him, and were old enough to always be able to remember him. All but one of her boys were married with children of their own. She often went to visit them or they'd come to see her, but one of the things that she enjoyed the most was when one of them would need a weekend alone with their wives and the little ones would stay with her. Hearing the noise, laughter, and pounding of feet running through her house made it seem so much quieter after they departed, than it was before they had come. Gretta never intruded upon her children, although there were time's when she would like to give them her piece of mind, she refrained. In the same token, if they asked for her advice, she was always more than eager. Gretta hoped that they would never have any more anguish in their lives, but surprisingly she had never become over-protective with them, especially when each one of them left home. They admired that about their mother, which kept them closer to her.

As Gretta opened the oven, to check on the bread, she heard footsteps softly coming down the stairs. As she threw the dish towel over her shoulder, she shut the oven door as she straightened. Sally had a bewildered look on her face and understandably so. "Why dear, you haven't slept but an hour?" Gretta frowned.

"I know, but honestly I feel rested. My, my," as she swept her eyes around the kitchen, "Charles and Sydney are certainly going to know something's up. Why this kitchen hasn't sparkled, nor smelled this good in, well, *never*! That delicious aroma is the culprit for waking me up, my stomach is growling so loud, I was afraid that the neighbors on the other side of us were going to complain!" Sally said with a big grin.

Gretta thought that the nap that Sally had had, along with her bath, had done wonders for her. It was as if she were a different person. As that thought occurred to Gretta, she suddenly had the fear that Sally wasn't feeling better at all, that maybe she had pushed it all away and was in denial. Gretta searched Sally's face to confirm her fears.

As Sally caught the look, she spoke as she sat down heavily in one of the chairs. "Don't worry, Gretta, I know what you're thinking. I haven't forgotten anything, I just, well, I really can't understand it myself, let alone describe it to you. I just feel very peaceful and capable of dealing with what I need to deal with. Maybe it's because I let it *all out* earlier. I don't know, this is quite unexpected really. I do know that having you here, has been monumental in having someone to lean on and talk to."

As Gretta found a cutting board, she opened the oven and pulled out the warm, golden brown loaf of bread. She began slicing it into nice thick pieces, as she had done the tomatoes. After generously spreading them with butter that melted into the bread on contact, she brought the plate of sliced tomatoes, bread, salt and pepper shaker, and the roll of paper towels to the table. After grabbing two smaller plates and setting one in front of Sally, she sat down with a slight groan. "Well, dig in. We don't need table manners when it's just the two of us, do we?" Sally smiled gratefully at Gretta, as she helped herself.

They both sat there quietly, eating their tomato sandwiches with more enthusiasm than they would if they were taking their very first bite of a delicious lobster. After they had both devoured their first helping, they started talking. Gretta told Sally of her and John's talk when she was feeling angry and of his words to her. Neither one of them danced around the issue, they confronted it. Sally began talking about how she would handle her situation and absorbed all of Gretta's thoughts on the subject.

Gretta had always been right to the point with Sally, as Sally was with her. They had never been shy with each other and weren't going to start now. As John was with her, Gretta was tough, but not harsh. Sally asked her a lot of questions that Gretta sometimes didn't have answers to. Sally would ask Gretta if she should do this or that and Gretta only would respond by saying that she would know what to do, if and when that time came. Although Sally knew that Gretta was right, she still found herself wanting the answers to her questions now, rather than later.

Gretta had her belief in God, but she was never pushy about it to others. Although, when she was asked how she handled life's tragedies and could still smile, she would be honest and upfront about how her faith pulled her through. Not only did her faith just get her through life's rough patches, but it had picked her up, brushed her off, and always left her feeling good as new. So when Sally asked Gretta to pray with her, Gretta felt honored and took hold of Sally's hands as they prayed. As Gretta was asking God to open up Sally's heart, tears started trickling down Sally's face, without any of the shame or despair that they had had earlier. Afterwards, they were both silent for a bit.

As Gretta looked into Sally's eyes with the concern of a mother, she asked, "Sally, are you okay?"

With a small smile, Sally responded, "Gretta, do you know how good you feel when it's really hot outside and you're all sweaty and dirty from working in your garden, then go in to take a shower? Then afterwards, you feel so good and clean? Well, that's how I feel right now. I feel stronger, cleaner, as if I have washed away all those dirty, grimy feelings inside of me and have replaced them with peace and comfort. I feel as if I can handle anything that comes my way!" Sally laughed at her last statement. "Well, I guess I already am, aren't I? Gee, I hope that this is the biggest thing that's going to be thrown my way! Can't say that I start small, can I? At least, I'm starting *big, really big!*" Sally started giggling and they both started laughing, as if it were the funniest joke that they had ever heard.

"Gretta, I don't know how to express to you the immense gratitude I feel in my heart. And the roses, they are so incredibly beautiful. I know that it's going to take a little time, before I will really be able to get my mind around the fact that I'm going to die. Only yesterday, my major concern was what to get at the grocery store for dinner. It's not that I ever thought that I would live for ever or anything like that. It's, it's just always seemed so very far away. I just suspected that Charles and I would have a very long, fulfilling life then we'd just go naturally. Boy, this has really taught me a thing or two about the ole 'rose colored glasses.' I wish I could just keep this peaceful feeling with me all of the time. But honestly, Gretta, I'll be just fine and thank you again, for picking up the remnants of my tantrum. Mostly, just thank you for being my very dearest friend I have no idea what kind of helter-skelter I would have committed, had you not shown up then. Speaking of which, why did you stop over here, anyhow?"

Gretta reddened a shade, "You know, Sally, I don't have the slightest clue. Isn't that odd? Ah, yes, now I remember. God told me that if I didn't get my hiney over here quick, that I was going to have a *full* day of cleaning, instead of just an hour or two!" as she joked with Sally. "Now, are you sure you don't want me to stay for a while?" Gretta asked in a more serious tone.

"I'm absolutely positive Gretta. I need some time to think about how I should approach Charles and Sydney with this news. I don't really think that I have it in me to tell them today, or even tomorrow, for that matter. I'm hoping to keep everything as normal as possible for as long as possible."

"Sally, just don't overlook the fact that Charles and Sydney also need time to prepare, just as you do. Plus, I'm afraid that you may make them feel cheated if you don't tell them until things are impossible to hide anymore. This time with your family is very precious, each and every minute is important.

They will remember this for the rest of their lives, as I do with John's last days. I only wish I wouldn't have wasted a moment, as I did. I will forever regret that, too. I know it will be painful for you to tell them, as it will be painful for them to hear it, but you must. It's beneficial for all of you, because you'll have them to lean on, as they will have you to lean on. I know that there will still be days filled with every single emotion you can possibly imagine and some that you may not. Believe me, Sally, I know that you have faith and that you go to church every Sunday, *but* this is a time that you can *really* get to know your Lord. Allow Him to fill you with peace, strength, and love, not only allow it, *but demand it*! He's with us always, but many don't think so, because they never allow Him into their lives. Instead, He stands at the door of our hearts as a mannerly visitor would do, until He is asked to come in. I used to make Him wait, in fact, most people do. They keep that door shut tighter than a drum, but then *whammo*! They find themselves in some kind of agony, pain, depression, or trouble, then who do they beg and plead with for help? Always seeming to promise that they will do this or that, if only He will grant them this one wish, as if He were some sort of genie in a bottle! They don't see that they never had to beg or plead with Him for help in the first place, for He was there all the time. They don't realize that they don't have to barter with Him. He's not a vendor at a flea market, trading His wares for ours, besides we could never afford all that He offers us anyhow. He gives it to us freely, willingly. In fact, He can't wait to give it to us. So even after we have broken those long forgotten promises we had made to Him, the Lord still doesn't leave. Nope, all He does is step back out the door of our hearts that we close to Him again, and wait until He's allowed back inside."

"You know, Gretta, it's ironic, because right now I'm so angry at God for doing this to me. *To my body!* All I keep thinking is what possible reason is there! I've always tried to be a good person, I've never asked for much from him? Why does he have to do this to Charles and Sydney? What on earth could they have done to have to be hurt like this? *What have I done to be hurt like this?* Gretta, is it that I haven't been grateful enough for the things that I have? Is it the fact that things were just rolling down the road just fine that he wanted to throw a wrench in our lives? Were we too happy, too content, too hardworking, *too anything?* Or maybe it's just that he's bored, so we happened to be the poor wretches that were in the wrong place, at the wrong time? I know, I know . . . I can whine, moan, cry, beg, scream, and ask *why, why, why,* till I'm blue in the face and that's all I'll get in return, *is just that, blue in the face!* Don't worry, Gretta, I'm not sliding back down that deep dark hole that I was in when you first arrived. Yes, I'm feeling sorry for myself. Yes, I'm mad. Yes, I want some answers, but I am *not* slipping. Can you understand what it is I'm trying to say? I just think that it's ironic that the one I'm so angry at right this very instant is the same one I should have trust in, and leaning on. Doesn't that sound kind of strange to you?" Sally pleaded.

"Yes, Sally, but what I also know is that sometimes things occur in our lifetimes that we will never have answers for. That is not what God wants us to do with our lives. What we have been through, our experiences, good or bad, painful or painless, what He expects from our lives, is to *grow, mature, learn, and finally ripen,* so that He can take us to His home. This is kind of a practice; it's nothing like we can ever imagine when we finally sit at the place the Lord has set for us at His table. As hard as it is, instances like these are not supposed to be easy, or magically disappear, but they are teaching us. How we use the things that we have learned is the true test, Sally. I have found when I'm focused on a certain object, that's what I'm seeing. So when you don't like what you are seeing, change your focus.

So by continuing to focus on your bitterness, resentment, and anger, that is what you will see and feel. For instance, some people only learn hatred, anger, distrust, and revenge. That's not learning anything at all, that's only *reacting*."

"You see, the easier things become in our lives, the more difficult the *easy* things become. Nothing about life is easy, nor was it meant to be. Although, I still often wonder about other's suffering, why it seems some have so much more heartache than others. So I do understand what you're saying. I think that maybe you're feeling somewhat sabotaged by the person that you trusted. I remember feeling the same way when this happened to John. There was no way that I was going to be *forced*, and I don't use that term loosely. I wondered why I should be *forced* to believe in the One, who had caused me so much pain and anguish. I felt as if I had been cornered by God. I felt as if He were being arrogant. It was as if He was dangling all His power in my face, just to make sure I knew who the boss was. Sally, I wish I could give you some kind of reasonable answer, but I honestly don't have any. All I do know is that since I've let go of the anger towards Him and come to trust *in Him*, I am at peace. It's like closing your eyes and letting yourself fall back, while totally relying on the person behind you to catch you and not let you get hurt. It's not an easy thing to do, but it is possible to achieve. Actually, it feels pretty darn good to hand over all of your fears, burdens, and troubles, and just say, *here ya go Big Guy*! *It's all yours, now you take care of it*! I no longer feel guilty asking for anything from Him; it's what He wants. He wants to take care of us. He wants us to be happy, peaceful, and free from pain. We still get caught in storms, but we have a new confidence that we'll get through it. This is how I've learned to deal with the questions that you're asking. John helped me with this one and it made enough sense to me, to believe it. John felt *lucky* that God had chosen to take him when he did, *can you believe that?* I thought John had gone certifiably *crazy*. Well, I still think he was, in fact, crazy that is, but on the other hand, this is how John expressed to me, all the 'why's.' God made each and every single one of us. We matter to Him. He placed us on this earth for a purpose that was designated distinctly for us. We have an ability to learn and to use what we have learned. You learn from the time that you're an infant and never ever stop, whether you want to or not. In fact, that was John's way of making light of our circumstances. He would often tell me, when I'd argue a point with him, that he had been chosen because he had learned everything there was to learn. So instead of having to trudge through life as an elderly man, with all the usual aches and pains that went along with it, he got to skip a few grades," Gretta said with a little laugh as she drew that particular memory out of her file.

Sally wished she had even a thimble full of the optimistic way of looking at things, as John seemed to have. Then her situation wouldn't seem so dire. She still had the 'ole standby, self-pity, lurking around for that one little tiny opening that it needed to get back inside. Just when self-pity thought it had found an opening, Sally changed her focus.

"Would you just look at the time. You've been here all day long Gretta, giving me all of your free time, cleaning up my tantrums, and feeding me, not only food, but some very good advice. Then you almost get out of here and I start my foolishness all over again. You'd think that I was the first one and the only one in this world diagnosed with terminal cancer. There are children who seem to be better equipped to deal with it than I am. Listen Gretta, you go on and get out of here. I'm going to gather my wits together and just play it by ear." Sally gave her a quick hug, before turning her to the door.

"You know if you need . . ."

"I know, I know. Gretta?" Sally said after cutting her off.

Gretta turned to Sally, waiting. "Gretta, I just wanted to tell you that I love you as if you were my sister and that your friendship to me has been very important and a wonderful gift."

"No need to start getting all mushy now! Besides, it's quite apparent, anyhow. Okay?"

Sally just smiled at Gretta's embarrassment. Sometimes Gretta could be so unpredictable, one minute she's crying and laughing with you, and the next, she's brushing you off, when it gets too mushy for her. *One just never knew, with her,* Sally thought as she watched this woman in her 60's, walk back to her home, as if she were only 20 years old.

Sally sighed deeply, as she watched Gretta. She leaned on the door frame for a moment and crossed her arms. With angst, she felt a twinge of jealousy towards Gretta. Immediately, Sally felt guilty for the brief thought that she had. Sally watched her until she disappeared inside of her home, then stood in the doorway and looked at her front yard, as if seeing it for the first time. How really beautiful it was, with her one "messy" weeping willow standing there, looking strong and sturdy, until you looked at it's branches. They seemed to look as if they were oh so very tired and defeated with their branches bending low, but that was what gave it those two appearances, one of vulnerability and the other, of strength. One without the other wouldn't look natural anymore, nor would it survive alone if someone were to separate them. Sally slowly closed the front door.

Sally turned and walked back through the living room to the kitchen, where she grabbed the long yellow legal pad that she often used to jot reminders and notes to herself about any bookkeeping concerns that she had and needed to ask Charles about. She didn't interrupt his day with her questions, so she would just run to the shop and look into it herself, unless it was something she couldn't find.

CHAPTER *ten*

When they were newlyweds, Charles couldn't wait to open his own shop. He had always dreamed of owning his own, rather than have to work underneath someone else, without the freedom of putting his own creativity to work. Charles hired a couple of young guys, mostly to do some of the mundane tasks, like oil changes, flat tires, tire rotations, etc. Charles biggest dream was to become one of the best, as far as "relics," "hot rods," and "souped up" vehicles. He could do it all; he painted, trimmed, and rebuilt the engines from square one. It was time consuming and required an extreme amount of patience and perfectionism.

Charles sometimes would forget the time and work until he couldn't keep his eyes open anymore. This had caused quite a few arguments in the fetal stages of their marriage. Sally was still insecure and couldn't understand why he preferred to work so late into the night, rather than be with her, so she took it as a direct insult. But Charles, on the other hand, was oblivious as to why Sally would be so hurt and angry with him all the time. He couldn't understand why she was upset and also felt she was inhibiting him, just as much as if he were working for a boss again. So, it had become inevitable that things were warming as a volcano, getting ready to erupt. And they did one evening, but not at all in the way he anticipated.

Charles had come home after another unusually long day, but he had completed the car and was in a celebratory mood. He was extremely proud of the work he had done on this particular car and didn't need anyone else to tell him how good it was. It had turned out perfectly, thankfully, because this was one of his most desired customers. He knew that if he pleased this particular fellow that he was *in like flynn*.

He had called Mike just as he was getting ready to leave the shop to tell him that his vehicle was ready. After bragging with him about how "sweet" it looked, Mike asked him if he would mind hanging out just a little longer, so that he could view it for himself. Mike was just as enthusiastic about cars as was Charles, but didn't have the talent that Charles did; instead, he had the money to pay for what he wanted. Charles agreed, of course, his excitement would be dampened again he was sure, when he arrived at home, because Sally didn't feel the enthusiasm that Charles did. Actually, if he wanted to be honest with himself, she had zip, zero, nil nothing even close to sharing the pride in his achievements. Sally, on one hand, just didn't have the capacity to understand why a *car* could bring such happiness to him and she couldn't. It was almost akin to another woman for Sally. She felt the same feelings, in the aspect that he put his business before her and felt hurt, insulted, jealous, and lonely. Charles didn't see it that way at all. He felt all of the exact same feelings that Sally was feeling, hurt, insulted, and lonely, because Sally didn't show one iota of interest to something that he had spent his whole life dreaming of and working towards.

He wasn't going to fail and in order to become the best, he had to build a clientele and please them. The one's that respected his work were the very one's that would keep him successful, because those were the one's who would return. They had the means to enjoy their hobby, but didn't have near the amount of experience and creativity that Charles did. Not only did Charles want her to share in the success of the business, but he felt proud of the fact that he was providing for not only their basic needs, but over and above that. She would never want for anything, she wouldn't have to worry about making the mortgage, how much she was spending at the stores, and more than anything, he wouldn't ever have to hear those dreaded words, "I don't have anything to wear!" He had wanted to give her a carefree life, so why in the world was she so angry all the time?

Every time he stayed late anymore, it was only because he couldn't quit in the middle of what he was doing, which caused Charles a bit of resentment towards Sally. Their arguments had become wearisome. They always began and ended the same way. Neither one of them took the time to really listen to the other, to find any sort of resolution towards a happy medium. Even though Charles had started leaving a specific time each night from the shop, he would also bring home his resentment at not being able to stay if he needed to. But the tension was far more frightening to him than losing his business. The air seemed to become so thick with tension, at times, that he felt he could slice it with a butter knife.

Tonight, though, he stayed, not because he couldn't leave, but because he was so close to being done that he didn't want to wait until the next day to see the finished product. This one night certainly wasn't much to ask . . . after all, she hadn't had to compromise anything. So he did, not arriving home till almost 9:00 p.m. Even though his day had started at 6:00 a.m. and he hadn't had any significant breaks during the day, he felt energized. Mike was more than pleased with his work. Charles felt as if he had been given validation, *finally*! Charles stopped at the store to pick up some flowers to bring home, deciding that this mutiny between them was going to end. When Mike wrote him the check that evening, he didn't mention one word about how come it cost so much. But when he handed it to Charles he told him, "You get what you pay for, Charlie 'ole boy, and I can't wait to get this thing on the road to show her off. She's a beauty, thanks," as he gave Charles a pat on the back. At that moment, Charles finally felt he had gotten a return on all of the hard work he had put in and felt a flicker of relief at being able to finally exhale, as if he had been holding his breath this whole time.

As Charles pulled into the driveway, he noted that it looked as if Sally had already gone to bed, because there were no downstairs lights on. While he was waiting for the garage door to go up, he glanced at the flowers that he had bought, hoping against hope that those paired with the biggest smile and hug he could manage just might soften her undoubtedly bad mood to a simmer. Taking a big breath, he lumbered out of the car with his purchase and prepared himself to keep his cool, rather than allowing himself to lose control of his anger as he often did. They had both become accustomed to the harsh words that each would fling back and forth at each other; that in the beginning was only a barely visible crack, but now had become a chasm between them. Neither one of them, while absorbed in their anger, realized how dangerously close they were getting to the edge.

As Charles walked into the house, he was startled to find his wife sitting in the living room, looking absolutely beautiful, with candles lit above the fireplace. She had the stereo on low, with some soft, lilting music playing. Charles was totally confused; he had readied himself for her aggression, but she had turned the tables on him and he was unprepared. *Would he ever know what to expect from this woman he married?* Charles wondered as he stood there feeling at a loss for what he should do now.

Sally enjoyed the discomfort that Charles was in, so she took her time in saying or doing anything and just basked in the moment. She knew that Charles had fully intended to come home and expect another argument from her, but he had been trying so hard to be home earlier and to appease her. She, too, felt the tension, even when he did exactly what she wanted him to do. But even so, she still expected him to do more. After he started coming home earlier, she still had behaved the same way. She expected him to read her mind and devote his undivided attention to her. When she didn't receive this, she became angry, but when Charles would ask her if she were upset about something, she'd be short and obviously not happy, but still told him no.

Sally was as tired of this as was Charles, so she had spent the last couple of weeks doing some real soul searching. She even went to the local library and checked out some books on relationships, how to make one work, how to keep one exciting, etc. She would always hide them before Charles came home, for fear that he would realize that she actually cared that much about their life together; for in her mind, if he knew of her fear of losing him that would leave her vulnerable and leave him with the control. While reading the last one, she realized that it was that kind of attitude that would be the fatal wound of their relationship. Basically, she realized that in order to hold this marriage together, *she*, not he, would have to get moving. He was willing to compromise and meet her, not just half way, but as far as he needed to go. She, on the other hand, had just stood there, not just stood there, but even backed up a few paces to see how far he would go to meet her expectations. She knew that she would eventually wear him down to where he'd do exactly what she anticipated he'd do, which was to confirm her fears of not loving her enough and just give up. She and Gretta had had many long discussions about her feelings. Gretta was the one, surprisingly, to say how disappointed she was in Sally.

"Sally, I think that I've spent about all the time that I will allow discussing an issue that will never see a resolution. I've told you my thoughts on both sides, but it seems to me that every single time I say something about your *negative* actions that need to be worked on, it's as if you totally shut down. Oh sure, you nod and act as if you're listening to me, but if you are, *then you certainly aren't hearing or understanding me correctly.* You don't want to fix anything as far as I can see, you just want someone to agree with you and tell you that you are right. Well you're not, you're wrong. That man has been working his tail end off for you. I understand you feel he's neglecting you, when in all actuality he's doing the total opposite. Men are different than women. He's showing you how much he loves you by trying to provide you with anything you want, but he's ignorant to the fact that it's not *things* that you want, *it's him.* Well, stop treating him like he's one of us! He's a *man*, so therefore, the *only* way you'll ever get the thing that you desire is to step up to the plate and get it yourself. I've listened to you whine, moan, groan, and complain for weeks now, about how your husband doesn't love you enough, about how you never get to see him, about how his hours spent at work has been putting stress on your relationship, and on and on it goes! All I'm hearing is me, me, me, and me. My God, how many other women I know that would give *anything* to have your complaints. Do you actually *hear* what you're saying? I mean, come on Sally, enough's enough. If he were home all the time, you'd probably be whining about how he's always in the way, why doesn't he get out of your hair more, why doesn't he give you time to yourself, etc. There are always things to complain about, but there are also things to be glad about.

"I want you to tell me exactly what have you done to alleviate this supposedly 'sinking ship'? No, never mind, I already know the answer, you've whined about it and yelled about it, but you haven't tried one single solution to solve it. Tell me, Sally, what do you think would have happened had you handled this so called 'problem' differently, rather than feeding it? By feeding it, you have caused it to grow into something so big, that you soon won't be able to pull the roots out, no matter how long, hard, or deep that you dig. Because it will have grown for so long and become so strong, that the roots have become so very deeply embedded, that it becomes impossible to remove them all?" Gretta sat there with her arms crossed across her chest, her legs crossed, and her face held an expectant expression on it.

"Why, I'm not sure I know what you mean?" as Sally's wall started to rise up again. Sally felt unfairly accused of being the bad guy. She felt like Gretta was blaming her and was angry because of it. Right then, she didn't like Gretta so much and wished that she had never said a word. Sally almost felt as if asking Gretta to leave. *After all, how dare she come into my home and tell me that I've brought all of this onto myself!* Sally thought to herself as she looked at this woman who sat in *her* home, perched on the chair, with such a self righteous look.

Sally's discomfort was written all over her face. Gretta wanted to pull that anger out of Sally. Whenever Sally became uncomfortable or too vulnerable at getting hurt, she'd pull that anger out and use it as a shield. Gretta had seen how well it worked for her, but she wanted her to use it with her, so that she could show her that it wasn't a shield at all, it had become her weapon, and weapons are used to harm, maim, and kill.

Sally pushed people away when she felt too close to feeling hurt. Everyone treated Sally with *kid gloves*, always afraid of upsetting her. It gave her some sort of power, but it was no longer a positive thing. In some situations, it's a good thing to have, but not all situations. Charles was probably one of the worst. It wasn't that he was a weak man, just that for some reason he thought that his wife was very fragile and would break if she didn't get her way. But then again, as she had told Sally, he was, after all, *a man*. Gretta didn't think that men were less than women, but after being married to John for many years, she found that they truly were different beings, their thought patterns, their emotions, and their way of expressing them. The most important thing to know about them was *that they will never* do what we want them to do on their own. Every now and again, they needed a few hints and nudges, and sometimes just a downright shove in the same direction as us.

Gretta finally spoke. "Sally, I realize that I sound like a know-it-all. To be honest, I feel that I do *know-it-all*, only because I was just like you when I was younger, but then, I slowly matured. I look back and wish I knew then what I know now, but then again, don't we all wish that? I'm not trying to be your enemy, but I would be, had I sat silent and let you bury your own marriage. Listen." Gretta uncrossed her arms and legs and leaned in, with her elbows resting on her knees, as she spoke. "I'm going to give you a hypothetical example. Now tell me honestly what you think would have changed your situation from what it has become to being something that never would have been a *situation* in the first place, had you, let's say . . . hhmm, instead of getting angry, would have thrown the dinner into your jeep, instead of the garbage, and drove it down to the shop, while Charles worked late?

"Did you think that he would turn you or that meal away? Well at least not the meal, anyhow!" Gretta joked. "He probably would have enjoyed some company. He might not have sat down to a table to eat, if he was involved in something, but he would find a way to get a bite in here or there. If I were him, I'd probably be a little miffed at you. I mean the whole reason for this mess started with a complaint from you that you weren't getting enough time with your *new husband*. But yet, you weren't so lonely that you felt compelled to drive to the shop and show him how much you missed him, did you? His appreciation at you going out of your way to bring him dinner and sit with him would have been a much clearer way of spelling out to him what it was you wanted.

"You instead used your anger to tell him that you missed him and he needed to be with you more. I'll bet now this is just an assumption on my part, but I'll bet you all the perfect men in the world that by changing your behavior just a little teeny tiny bit, his would have been different, too. The one night that you didn't show up with that nice warm meal and that sweet loving way you have every now and again would have made him realize that those cars were losing value, compared to you. That a few less dollars a month wouldn't add up to as much of a loss as the time with you would, if he lost it. If you ever want to become important to someone, you must show them on your own how really important you are to them. By giving all of the time, energy, and love you can dole out, to where they've become so dependant on it, it becomes something they don't want to live without, because it becomes a part of them and if they were to lose it, then they would lose a part of themselves. *Love begets love and hate begets hate*, my dear. So tell me, which of those do you choose to have in your life? No matter which one it is, whatever you choose, then you're gonna have to give some, to get some; it's as simple as that! No big secret to unravel, no scientific definition, and no Einstein to invent it. So right now, let's think for a moment, hhmm . . . are you getting back what you're giving? Yep, indeed you are, but it's not what you want; so *my dear Watson*, how are you going to get from Charles, the desired response?"

Sally lost the "shield" that she had been preparing to pull out earlier. "Okay, uncle!" Sally mocked while raising her hands up in surrender. "I give, okay? I'll give it a try, but if it doesn't work, you have to show me where *even one perfect man is!*"

"Uh, I think he's working right now," Gretta winked, as she got up and stretched out her limbs. "You know what I think?"

Still laughing, Sally asked, "No Gretta, I don't think I'll ever know what you think, of course, until you tell me, like you have this afternoon."

"Your quick, I like that. But anyhow, I think that if I had gone on to become a marital therapist, I'd be dirt poor."

"I guess I really don't understand, Gretta, why would you be poor? From what I hear they make a killing!"

"Oh, I wouldn't. I wouldn't be able to draw it out for weeks and weeks as they do. I've got you all fixed in less than an hour. I'd just be too good for my own benefit. Of course, instead of charging hourly, I could just charge one flat fee, without having to waste anyone's time, huh?"

"Wow, you're feeling quite full of yourself, aren't you? Don't go getting all high and mighty yet, after all, I could still get served divorce papers this afternoon, you know, and then what?"

"Ha, but if it does happen then you're going to have to resort to begging. On that my dear, I have no promises on how that will work. I've gotta get out of here. I've got a lot to do today, before my date arrives this evening," as she flung her hand out haughtily, like a prima donna.

"Ah, yes, the social butterfly probably needs a brief respite from the date that she had last night! I just thought of something! No wonder you know so much about men, you've gone through almost all of them around here. In fact Gretta, you're going to have to pack up and leave before long, because you're running out of material!"

"Very funny, but now that you mention it, it is a point to ponder," as she exited quickly out the back door laughing all the way.

So as Charles stood there, looking dumbfounded at Sally, still clutching the flowers that he'd bought for her. Sally couldn't keep herself from laughing. It was almost as if Charles felt that he had gone to the wrong home, for this behavioral change in his wife was so unlike the last few weeks, even while it being a good thing, it took him by complete surprise. "Pretty flowers, Charles, but if you don't loosen that grip on them, you'll choke them to death."

Charles looked down at the flowers that he had in his hand, as if he didn't know how they got there. "I, uh, brought these flowers home for you." As he looked from her to the candles, he had a fleeting moment of terror, thinking he may have forgotten an important date, as his brain started running through birthdays, holidays, anniversaries, etc., but nothing came up.

It was as if Sally had read his mind. "I'm sure you're wondering about all of this." Sally started to feel embarrassed that maybe she had gone overboard by the reaction she was getting from him. As she started to nervously explain to him that it was an appeal for forgiveness for her selfish behavior, Charles moved to her, cutting her off with a kiss, while feeling weeks and weeks of tension start to melt away, replaced with relief, joy, and the wonder at how they could have possibly forgotten this exquisite, beautiful feeling, of love for one another.

CHAPTER *eleven*

How right Gretta was, Sally thought to her self, as she stood there holding the legal pad, with that memory standing out. She and Charles got over that first hump in their marriage and learning from that made any other's that arose seem trivial. That was how she became the bookkeeper for his shop. She would occasionally drop into the shop during the day if she were out running errands, and on one particular day, while he was elbow deep in grease, the phone rang and she answered it. It was one of the supplier's that he had ordered parts from and they were inquiring about whether he had already sent his payment in or not, and if so, then when could they expect one. After searching through the piles and piles of paperwork he had strewn all over his desk, she had found the invoice, with a small piece of paper stapled to the corner, stating the check number, amount, and date. Sally found herself shaking her head two and a half hours later, still amidst a state of chaos, but it wasn't quite as big as it was earlier. She had been trying to organize everything into incoming, outgoing, then into smaller piles separated alphabetically, still amazed that Charles was able to keep things going as smoothly as they seemed to be going with his kind of filing system.

Charles had come sauntering into the office that day, finding Sally with her back to him at his filing cabinet, placing some paperwork into one of the file folders that were obviously empty. "Are you still here? I thought that you left a long time ago?"

As Sally turned around, she looked frazzled. "Well, I would have left along time ago, but after spending almost a half an hour on the phone with one of your suppliers, and trust me, it wasn't because of them, it was because of this." As she splayed her arms out, nodding towards the nice neat piles sitting on his desk, waiting to be placed into their new home. "How on earth can you keep track of anything in this office? It would drive me completely nuts!"

"Would? It seems it drives you nuts, anyhow. Now, since I don't want anything driving my sweet anywhere and you've put everything into some kind of order, I'm sure that now *I'll never be able to find it*! There was a method to my madness, you know. If you would have just hollered at me, I would have found it right away."

"Yeah, kind of like you can find your clothes when you get home, lying all over the floor, where you left them the night before?"

"They're not on the floor?"

"That's because this wonderful little fairy, that you like to call your *wife*, picks them up and washes them, then she places them nice and neat into the drawer where they belong."

"Yeah, I guess you're right. And since you have been so good at that, why don't you give this a whirl?"

He's actually serious! "I, um, I don't think so, Charles. I mean, well, you probably really should have someone that has experience in this kind of work."

"Hhmm, now let me see, you obviously know how to file, I mean that is what you're doing right now, isn't it? And I know that you can type, add and subtract, write checks, and put up with a mean, domineering boss, whom I might add, likes his coffee with cream and sugar. You also know what I like for breakfast, eggs over, hash browns and bacon both cooked crisp and whole wheat buttered toast every morning, topped off with a nice delicious kiss! Seriously Sally, I've really been needing someone to help in the office, the pay's not terrific right now, but it'd be perfect for us. You've been talking about getting a job, anyhow? Why not this? I know it's not quite what you've had in mind, but can't you just try it for a little while? For no other reason than to hold me through till I can find someone else to do it?"

How can I say no? He knows just how to work me? "Okay, okay, but it'll only be a temporary thing for right now; this is just until you can find the proper person to hire!"

"Fine, now lets shake on it." He smiled.

Well, that particular afternoon turned into quite a long one for Sally. She ended up staying the rest of the afternoon with Charles, trying to finish what she had started, and start what Charles had left to be finished. She was so hunkered down that when Charles finally came in the office to tell her it was quitting time she had no idea of the hour. As she looked at her wrist watch, she was amazed that it was 8 p.m. in the evening already.

"Come on, little lady, even Rome wasn't built in a day? Why don't I take my new *employee* out for dinner, since she's worked so hard her first day on the job? I just hope that my wife doesn't find out that I'm going out to dinner with my new secretary." He snickered.

"I promise not to tell her, as long as you take me somewhere nice and very, very expensive," as she led him out the door.

I don't think that he ever even looked for anyone. Sally smiled to herself with the memories. As she slowly brought herself back to the moment, she wondered how long it would be, before she could believe her diagnosis was real. It would sink in slowly, as rain does to the bottom of a dry desert floor.

I can't tell him tonight. Sally thought as she looked at the long, empty sheet of yellow paper sitting in front of her, with her pen posed, waiting for a command from her to begin. She instead dropped it down on top of the pad with frustration, as she leaned back in the chair as she roughly ran her fingers through her hair. She looked up at the clock on the wall of the kitchen and decided that she wasn't going to spend her time worrying about just that very thing, *time.*

CHAPTER *twelve*

Sally ended up never having to find the right words to tell her husband Charles. For the following week, while she and Charles were getting ready for bed after Sydney had fallen asleep, she felt an excruciating stab of pain through her body, as if someone were stabbing her with a hot poker. As she doubled over, Charles sat straight up in bed; he jumped out as quickly as he could. She couldn't register what Charles was saying to her, as her pain seemed to demand her full attention. After she felt it ease up a bit, she sat down on the edge of the bed and finally was able to see the anxiety on Charles face.

He had become angry, *"I'm going to call that doctor and find out why he hasn't called us back yet with the results of all those tests that he took on you! For crying out loud, it's been almost two weeks now! He sure better have some answers or he's going to answer to me! I won't sit by and watch you go through all this pain."*

Suddenly he absorbed the look on her face and stated, rather than asked, "The doctor has called you? Sally, please answer me," he pleaded softly as he knelt down in front of her, taking her face into his hands, not allowing her to avoid his eyes.

Sally felt weak, not so much from the recent spasm of pain,

but from having to face the truth with Charles. She started to feel that by not telling him, it wasn't true, but finally being unable to squirm out of it this time made it feel so final. As that feeling came over her, she started to cry. "I'm so sorry, I'm so sorry, Charles. This is my fault! Oh Charles, I'm so scared!"

Charles was still not quite sure as to what she was talking about, but felt an unaccustomed feeling of fear tighten his stomach. "Sally, what is it? What's your fault? What is it that you're afraid of? I don't understand, Sally talk to me please tell me what's going on!"

"The doctor called me last Tuesday and wanted me to come in to see him on Wednesday, to talk with him about my results. I think I knew it wouldn't be good, because he asked that I bring you with me. But I didn't want you to worry, or maybe it was because I thought that if I went alone I would be able to handle it better. I, I . . . gu . . . guess I don't really know why I didn't want you to know. He told me that I've got cancer. S'pose I suspected that, but I never th . . . thought that it was or could be this bad. I mean, I thought he was going to tell me that I would have to have a breast removed, and I think that's why I didn't tell you, because I was afraid, afraid that it would change us . . . or things between us, or how you felt about me. Now I wish that's the news he gave me, but instead I find out that no matter how many parts of me I have removed, it won't change the fact that it's terminal. He said that it's spread all throughout my body, it's too far gone, so the only hope that I had was not living a long life, but only being able to stay alive for only a few months. He gave me six months, tops, and I think that he was being optimistic at that!" She watched through her tears, her husband's face as she told him.

Charles couldn't move, his face had lost color, the beating of his heart gathered speed, and he had drops of sweat break out on his forehead; all were reactions to the sheer terror he was experiencing at the thought of losing Sally. He was stunned, while he felt his brain telling him to speak, his lips tried to form words, but his throat felt as if it had a vice around it and wouldn't allow any air through. His vision went blurry from the tears starting to form. So instead, he stood up and walked towards the staircase as quickly as he could, so that she wouldn't see him losing the composure that she needed so badly right now to lean on. For the first time in their marriage, he didn't think he had the strength to hold himself up, let alone her too. So as he practically ran down the stairs as quickly as he could, the only thing he could think of to help him regain that strength was the bottle of scotch that they had received from one of his friends on their wedding day, that had sat untouched and tucked away far back in the kitchen cabinet over the stove.

Sally, hesitantly, followed him down the stairs. By his response, she felt he was probably so angry at her, not for just keeping the doctor's appointment from him, but because she didn't go to see him much sooner. Her guilt had become so immense that after he left the bedroom without a word, she decided to follow him downstairs and throw all of her humility out and plead with him not to hate her. She wasn't quite as quick nor as nimble as he was, after her last episode, so that by the time she reached the kitchen, she found him downing a juice sized glass of scotch down as if it were a cold glass of water on a sweltering summer day. After he finished that one, he immediately poured another one and leaned his hip against the counter while searching for what he should say or do.

Sally watched him, knowing that he was very upset, because in all their years and battles, she had never once seen him drink a drop of alcohol. It was something that neither one of them had ever resorted to. Sally was surprised that he even remembered it was there, for it had sat untouched for so long that it was caked with dust.

Charles, for the first time in his life, was scared and didn't know what to do with this new horrid feeling that had reared its ugly head up. It seemed the moments of silence that had lapsed between them were more like eons. As he looked from her to the velvety gold liquid, swirling in his glass, he found himself wondering, as he looked back at his wife, how he could ever possibly live without her. *These last fifteen years I've spent on trying to get to the point to where we could lay back, relax, and enjoy the things that I've been working so hard to achieve. All these years, just so that we could enjoy each other, spend more time together, take vacations, and enjoy our daughter together, down the drain. All that time I've wasted, for time that will never be, instead of taking advantage of the moments I had, I gambled it all and lost. Money was always the reason . . . never having enough of it, then having enough of it and still wanting more. It's all become so pointless. What good is having it now going to do for me? What's it going to buy me now? Is it going to buy my wife's life back? Is it going to take this knife out of my heart? My dear God, help me, help her please help us.*

Sally gripped the back of the kitchen table chair and was the first one to break the ice. "Charles, I realize that this has been thrown at you. I know how furious you must be at me right now. If I would have just listened to you in the beginning and gone to the doctor right away, then we probably wouldn't be dealing with what we're dealing with right now. But the truth of the matter is, I didn't and we are forced to deal with it. I need your forgiveness, I need your love, and I need you most of all. I realize that all of this is still sinking in, for crying out loud, I'm still reeling from the news and I've known for a week now, and probably knew it deep down inside for even longer. But I need you to talk to me, help me to know where your head is at right now." As she finished, she could see all of the unspoken emotions flit across his face as if she were watching a slide show. In a softer tone, "Charles, this is not just about you and I, it's also about a young girl upstairs that has need's that far outweigh our own. She is the priority. We can't lose ourselves in this, and don't think for a moment that I don't want to just curl up into one big ball and feel sorry for myself, but she's kept me brave. Without her knowing it, she's given me courage and strength. She's given me the ability to cope with my demise. With all she's given me, I feel it's only fair to give her the least amount of hurt as we possibly can."

Charles set down his almost empty glass on the counter and went to her, encompassing her into his arms. "I'm the one that's sorry. I'm not quite sure this is really happening, and to be quite frank, don't want to be sure. I've so many emotions running through me right now that I can't possibly grasp just one. The first one, of course, is anger, but not at you, but at the unfairness of it all. The second one is a crushing fear that is so overwhelming that I'm afraid I can't control it and if I acknowledge it, it will overtake me. I want to scream, cry, crumble, and more than any other feeling, want to wish it away and reverse it!

"Sally, you've only found out one week ago and only talked to one doctor. How about if we get a second opinion, or even a third, fourth, and fifth? Maybe he's wrong, maybe it's not as bad as he's saying it is. Maybe there *is* something that can be done. Can't we try? Then, if the outcome is the same, we'll discuss what we need to deal with, okay?" Charles couldn't hide, nor stop, the tears from falling down his cheeks. He had always prided himself on being so strong, manly, and never shying away from anyone or anything that posed a threat.

Sally couldn't ever remember him breaking down, except when Sydney was born, but those tears were out of love and happiness, now they were from love and sadness. Sally could feel her heart being ripped out a piece at a time, while at the same time, feeling proud that she was strong enough to, for the very first time, allow her husband to lean on her, at such a crucial time.

CHAPTER *thirteen*

Sally remembered back to when Sydney was only two years old, she and Charles had wanted lots and lots of children. She had become pregnant, but miscarried, which had been devastating for both of them, but they had clung to each other without losing hope of still succeeding. Then Sally had become pregnant again. This time she not only miscarried, but Charles had come home from work to find her laying in the bathroom floor in a pool of her own blood with Sydney sitting on the floor beside her, red-faced and crying at the top of her lungs. Charles gathered both of them up and rushed her to the hospital as quickly as he could, without even thinking about waiting on an ambulance to arrive. They had had to do an emergency hysterectomy on her to control the hemorrhaging, in which Charles had to make the decision for, since it was a life or death matter and she was unconscious. Charles thought that he was going to lose Sally that day and made his decision without even a second's thought.

He knew how badly Sally wanted more children and how crushed she was by the first miscarriage. It had taken her some time to recover from that alone. He stayed by her bedside constantly, with Sydney being taken care of by Gretta. When Sally finally awoke, still somewhat groggy from the medication, she looked directly into his eyes and knew that this child, too, was gone. The sob that erupted from her started from her very core, so that he couldn't possibly tell her that not only had they again lost another child, but that she would never be able to have any hope of bearing another child again.

The guilt he felt at his decision, even knowing that there wasn't any other choice, was heart wrenching for him to withstand. He held her hands and wept with her, for not only their loss, but for the loss of their hopes and dreams of having any more children. It was more than he could bear, as he looked at the total despair that lined her face. After they had both become exhausted from expressing their grief, the nurse had arrived with some more pain medication and to look over Sally to make sure that everything was stable. While she was there, Charles had taken this opportunity to step out of the room to grab a cup of coffee and call Gretta to check in on Sydney to make sure that she was alright.

After Gretta's assurance that all was well and not to worry, he started to make his way back down the hallway to Sally's room. As he neared, he heard a blood-curdling cry come from within and ran in to see what had happened. The nurse looked at him with a beet red face and guilt written all over it.

"I . . . I'm . . . so very sorry, I had no idea that she didn't know yet."

The realization of what had just transpired only took milliseconds to kick in. The nurse had told Sally of her hysterectomy, without realizing that she didn't know yet. Sally was hysterical she was screaming and crying, all the while jerking so hard that she was causing her IV to come out.

The doctor came rushing in and ordered the nurse to control Sally's movement, so that he could give her a shot to calm her down and stop any further harm that she may cause to herself.

Charles remembered feeling such hatred at that poor nurse and wanted to literally take her by the head of the hair and drag her as far away from the room as possible, never ever having had that reaction towards another woman in his life. Looking back, he remembered how horrid it must have been for that nurse, for the doctor wasn't very understanding either. The nurse ended up running out of the room in tears, with the doctor giving Charles a grim look, trying to apologize for the damage that the nurse had unknowingly created.

Charles, finally, was able to take Sally home from the hospital, with the hope that when she was home and with Sydney that it would take her mind off of not being able to have any more children. For during the rest of Sally's duration at the hospital, she had become despondent. Much to his dismay, it didn't go away after arriving home; she had become worse. She hardly ever left the bedroom, never even changed nightgowns, much less, put on street clothes. She had stopped eating anything, slept all of the time and had gotten so bad that Charles wouldn't even leave Sydney at home with her alone. He'd either take Sydney with him to work or Gretta would watch her until he got home in the evening. The guilt that Charles had felt then was much like the guilt he was feeling now. Only then, he felt as if he had made a rash decision, even with the doctor's assurance that he had had no other options. Sally furthered his feelings of guilt, after arriving home from the hospital when she told him that he should have let her die, because she felt dead anyhow. That hurt him more than he could bear, but he was at a loss. He loved her so much and seeing her this way crushed him. He tried to be everything, mother and father for Sydney, tried to run and maintain the shop that was suffering from all that he had to deal with, and more than anything, be hopeful that Sally still loved him and Sydney.

Then Gretta again came into her life once again, with her *no nonsense* attitude to life's disappointments, to express her opinion to Sally. Sally was downstairs, in her nightgown, as usual, when Gretta appeared at the door asking if she could come in for a moment. Sally was miserable and weary and didn't like being caught off guard. And Sally certainly didn't feel like becoming friendly right then. But dear 'ole Gretta, didn't wait for an answer, nor did she care, just came barging in, as if it were normal for her.

Gretta cut right to the punch. "You look like crap."

Sally just nodded and shrugged her shoulders, responding sarcastically, "Don't really care, I'm not planning on entering a *beauty contest* any time in the near future, anyhow."

"Well dear, you wouldn't stand a chance, even if you were planning on it, judging by the way you look! You know, hon, you've been in this slump for a while now, and to be honest, you've used all your time up! I understand the hurt and pain that you must feel, *and* I even understand your self pity, but you have wallowed quite long enough. It isn't fair, it isn't right, and it's very, very sad. You seem to have forgotten something vitally important. You haven't lost all of your children; you have one that desperately need's their mama back. Sydney is still here, why treat her as if she's not? Why blame your husband and daughter for being here? Why make them feel as if they don't matter at all? You know, God's will is a funny thing. It's not always pleasant to the taste to endure what he puts on our plates and we're always seeking a reason for it, a valid one, one that we can comprehend. Well, with God, not everything is black and white, not everything is going to jump out and say *hey, this is why I've done this to you.* Do you want Sydney to learn to crumble every time something doesn't go according to her plan? Of course you don't. You are taking out on them your anger at God for taking away what *you* have wanted. What you are hanging on to are unfulfilled hopes and dreams that you aren't sure were even worth it! Young lady, your life was saved; use it wisely, enjoy the things that you *do have.* Not the ghosts that you may have had! You have to let go of all that anger that you are clutching to so tightly. You need to let the Lord take away your pain. Otherwise, it will end up eating at you until there is nothing left, but a shell of bitterness and broken hearts. Think of your anger as a pebble and think of yourself and your family as a pond that's as still as a mirror. When you throw your anger, which is the pebble into that pond, what happens? Why, it causes a ripple that moves until it hits the shore. Well, those ripples are affecting your family and upsetting the calm and serene feelings that we all strive to attain. Give them back their peace, Sally. If you can't get out of your *slump*, then leave and give them the chance to find the happiness that they deserve to have, without making them share the unhappiness that you seem to have found a haven in."

Sally was lost for words. Never would Charles have spoken to her so bluntly. And as for Sydney, she didn't even want to be around her mother.

"Listen dear I'm not trying to be cruel to you. For I love you as if you were one of my very own. I just know that you're losing control over beating the misery that is poisoning you' it's become toxic, not just for you, but has spread to those who are in contact with you. Your husband is exhausted, he is becoming depleted and the only thing that keeps him going is the guilt that you've been feeding him day after day after day. He had to make a choice and his choice was to either let you die or let you live. He wanted you to live, because he loves you, not because he wanted you to be absolutely miserable, so miserable, in fact, that you can't even cope with normal day to day activities. Such as getting out of bed, number one! How long of a sentence must you impose on this man, have for being punished for *loving you*! How long are you going to ignore your child, until she understands that she isn't worth a single thing, because she should have died too! Because that's definitely the signal she's getting from you. You're giving the one's that didn't make it more attention, than you are to the one that did and really needs your attention and love. Believe me, I know that the last person in this world that you want to trust right now is God, but you must, or you will not survive without Him, nor will your family. Let Him give you strength. Sally, think of it as a debt that God owes you. He owes it to you to give you the strength that you need to overcome the demons in your heart. You have had an integral part of your being taken away from you. Aren't you the least bit interested to see what He's going to replace it with? Those two children that you lost are not lost, but blessed. They're with Him and as my husband always told me, it's only our selfishness that we want them here with us, instead of a perfect place, where they will never know pain, sadness, grief, or anger. I'm sorry for preaching my beliefs to you, well not entirely, because I think you need to hear it, but it works. I promise you without a doubt! Give someone else the reins to your pain, sorrow, despair, and anger. You cannot continue blaming others for continuing to live, continuing to love, continuing to smile, and for continuing to care! It hurts me to see you wasting such precious time that could be used for such precious moments in your life.

"There you go, honey, it's only the first of many layers, but you'll feel tremendously lighter in the long run." Gretta held Sally. "Just let everything out. If you don't then you might just explode!" Gretta said with a smile.

"Gretta, I'm so ashamed. Not for right now, but for the way I've treated Charles. I wanted to make him hurt, I wanted to see how much he'd let me make him hurt, and then I wanted to make him hurt so much that he'd just give up and let me use that as yet another crutch to keep being angry. But you know what? He never wavered, he never bent, he never gave up on me, because his guilt was larger than my own. How will I repair the damage that I've created with not only him, but my very own little girl?"

"Number one, Charles guilt had nothing to do with why he stuck in there. It take's something far stronger to sustain that kind of patience and if I were to guess, I suspect that something would be love. Now dear, I'm sure that you've heard that old saying, "love conquers all." I've never seen that statement contradicted yet. You are a grown woman who is constantly, consistently, and *forever* seeking answers to questions where there are none. Stop asking questions and you won't need any answers, now will you? Pretend that you play the piano and can't read music; that you can only play by ear. Well, that's sometimes how life is to be played, by ear, by feelings, by experiencing, by learning from mistakes, by learning from other's mistakes, and by sensing the needs of another. You always seem to be looking for some sort of Rubik's cube to solve, but it's much simpler than that. The hardest part for us humans to do is to feel vulnerable; we don't like that feeling, because we're so used to feeling sure, that way we can avoid pain in our lives. As long as you don't give up those completely trusting feelings and love completely and unconditionally, you'll never be anything but a mere existence, without the ability to actually live a life without any regrets."

After saying their goodbyes and giving Sally a great big bear hug, Gretta left her to her thoughts. Sally had her arms wrapped around her middle as she turned to go back upstairs, finding it surprisingly difficult not to crawl back into her cocoon that she had wound so tightly around her. As she walked through the empty house, she realized that it had become like her, empty and quiet, no life emanated from it. Sally looked at the time and noticing that it was still before noon, she trotted up the stairs and turned the shower on. She had no idea how she would make things right, but she wasn't going to spend one more moment on them going wrong. This moment in time had forever changed her, it had affected all of them, but if nothing else, she had *learned* something from it. The shower felt as if it were washing away the bad feelings inside of her that she thought had become so much a part of her, that to remove them would leave an empty hole.

Still standing in the kitchen, with his arms around her, Sally came back to the moment at hand. *This is my chance to shine. Dear Lord, please give me the strength and courage I need, so that the pain and sadness of leaving this man that I love so very much and my little daughter, whom I cherish, turn into joy and happiness. I will not "wallow" this time. For goodness sakes, I don't have that kind of time anyhow.*

CHAPTER *fourteen*

Charles faced her with his hands on hers, begging her to tell him that this wasn't happening. If she could, she would have, but she couldn't, so she wanted him to believe, even if she herself didn't that there were no reason for sadness or tears. For it would only waste precious time.

Everything happened so quickly that it was hard for any of them to absorb. Sally's death happened far more rapidly than any of them expected. Soon after the knowledge of her disease, it seemed to worsen by the minute. Sally only made it just short of two months, much less than any of them had planned for. Gretta remembered one particular evening, soon after Charles and Sydney found out about Sally. She had been looking out of her kitchen window. It was much the same design as Charles and Sally's house, which faced into the back yard. She watched the three of them sitting on a blanket on the grass eating and laughing as if the world around them was invisible. Sydney's laughter was the most precious sound that evening. Gretta, in the beginning, didn't know if it was a good thing or a bad thing, but they told Sydney the news of her mother only after they had exhausted all of their other options. Finally, Sally put an end to it and told Charles that she did not want to spend anymore days of her life hoping for a miracle, because it only made it harder on all of them when their hopes were dashed.

Charles was devastated by his wife's death. As he watched Sally's deterioration race throughout her body with lightning speed, he had been so busy taking care of her and Sydney that he wasn't allowed time to feel the pain that he felt after her last breath. Sydney had gone to her room and closed the door. Charles sat in the living room, with his elbows on his knees and his head in his hands. He thought about finishing off the bottle of scotch that he had, but after grabbing it down from the cupboard and uncapping it, instead of pouring it into his glass he watched it swirl down the drain, leaving behind its scent. He stood over the sink staring down as if he were in a trance. All he wanted at that moment was his wife back. He couldn't wait for everyone to leave, but now that they had, leaving Sydney and him all alone, he didn't welcome the loneliness and pain that they had been replaced with.

If one more person told me how it was going to get easier with time or told me to call them if we needed anything at all, to call them anytime . . . I was going to pop! Sally, oh Sally, what am I going to do without you. We weren't finished yet! We had so much left to do together. Oh God, Sally! I worked so hard, spent all of that time trying to make more and more money, so that we'd be able to enjoy so many things that we dreamed about, that you dreamed about! Now look, it's all ruined. You left me with all of these dreams that went up in smoke when you left! I can't be a mother for Sydney, I don't even know how. She hasn't spoken a word to me since you've left! I don't know what to do here, Sally! I always thought that having plenty of money would be all I'd want in life. I always thought that with that I'd have everything I needed. How wrong I was.

Charles wiped away the last of his tears roughly with his shirt sleeve. He loosened the tie that he was wearing and unbuttoned his shirt a couple of notches, then grabbed his suit jacket off the back of the chair, shut off the lights and started up the stairs. The weariness he had made him feel as if his whole body had been filled with bricks. As he started down the hallway to his room, he stopped at the closed door and rapped lightly, softly asking Sydney if she was still awake. Just as he started to walk away, he heard footsteps then she opened the door.

She didn't speak, only stood there, waiting. Her golden eyes had such a great deep sadness in them, underneath the wet redness, caused from her recent tears. Her cheeks were splotched with red and her lips were trembling. Each and every one of her curly amber locks seemed to have chosen a different direction than the other, which made it look wild and unruly.

His heart broke even further, if possible, from the hurt and pain his little girl was dealing with. He wanted to take it away from her, he wished he could take it from her, and he felt so helpless at knowing that he couldn't. The look on her face seemed to say, "*So now what do we do, Dad?*"

"I'd like to sit down and talk to you, Syd, okay?"

She only answered with a nod of her head, as she turned towards her bed and sat down on the edge of it.

Charles grabbed her desk chair, turned it around, and threw his suit jacket on the corner of her bed. As they sat there facing each other, he searched for the words. With a deep breath, he began, as he leaned in towards Sydney.

"Syd, I, uh, well I'm just as scared, sad, and mad as you are? There's just us left now and I think we need to talk about it. I need you to help me, because I don't know a lot of things. There are a lot of things that your Mom did, that I'm going to have to learn how to do myself, so it's going to be kind of a bumpy ride for a while. I'm not the greatest cook, housekeeper, and laundry guy, but I'm going to do my best. I know that you're hurting inside, but your mom made me promise to tell you that she'll always be here," as Charles pointed to her heart. "She told me that she would watch over the both of us. I miss her too, Syd, real, real bad. I suppose I will forever miss her. I can imagine how you feel. Gosh, I don't understand any of this; I don't know how anyone can expect you to! All I know is that we're stuck with each other, kiddo. So I want you to talk to me, to tell me if you're feeling sad, bad, hurt, sick, or just anything *even happy*! Both of us are thinking that we'll never be happy again, but everyone keeps telling me that we will. We'll see, I suppose. Sydney, I guess the most important thing I wanted to tell you, is that I love you very, very much. There isn't anything in this world that you or anyone else could do that would ever make me stop loving you. There isn't anything that you should *ever* be afraid to ask me or tell me. We'll get through this; your mother promised me she'd help us too. We're going to have to take this day by day and see what works and what doesn't, but I think before long we'll be able to get it down pretty good? Don't you think so?"

Sydney sadly nodded and tried to give him a smile, as he patted her knee. "Come on, I'll tuck you in." He pulled down her blankets that still had the imprint of her lying on top of them. As she slowly crawled in and he tucked her in all the way up to her neck, he gave her a hug and a kiss goodnight. As he started for the door, he heard a soft whimper calling to him. She had jumped out of bed, with her arms wrapping around his neck as he bent down.

"Oh Daddy, I love you! I'm afraid that you're going to leave me, too, like mommy did. I *want* her back so bad. I never listened to her when she would tell me to clean my room, or to help her clean the house. Maybe that's why she got so sick? Daddy, she made me keep a secret from you, *but I should have told you, then you could have fixed everything like you always do!*" Sydney stammered through her tears.

Charles hadn't heard Sydney call him "daddy" since she

was just a small child. She always referred to him as dad. It made him nervous, because he was afraid that she was reverting. "Sydney, what secret are you talking about?"

"That day after I got home from school and the doctor called, to tell her to come in to see him. She told me not to tell you, because she said you didn't need to worry, because you were working too hard. But if I wouldn't have listened, you could have done something to save her! Then she wouldn't be *dead*!" As she screamed the word dead out, she almost became hysterical with waves upon waves of sobs tumbling over each other as waves pounding into shore. Sydney was already as tall as her mother at her young age, but Charles didn't realize how thin she had gotten until he put his arms around her, to calm her down.

He let her sob into his chest, while holding her and telling her it was okay. "Sydney, you didn't do anything wrong! I wish I could have done something, but I couldn't. No matter if you would have told me about the phone call or not! Don't you blame yourself *for anything*! Your mother got sick and couldn't get better; it's not *anyone's* fault, okay?" As he felt her sobs turn into whimpers, he turned her back towards her bed and tucked her in again, rubbing her hair off of her forehead as he gave her a kiss where his hand had been.

"Close your eyes and rest now. I'm going to stay right here in this chair while you fall asleep, okay?" As he watched the heaviness of her eyes win the battle over trying to stay awake, Charles sat there long after Sydney had fallen asleep. *She looks so much like her mother,* Charles thought as he sat there. He leaned in to brush the rest of the hair that had fallen over his daughter's forehead away. He gave her one last light kiss on her cheek as he softly walked out of her room, towards his own.

After he yanked his tie off, he sat on the edge of his own bed, looking around the bedroom. As he did, he saw Sally's touch everywhere. Even the dresser sitting in their room brought memories back to him from when they were first married. He remembered them arguing about that big, bulky, old dresser. It had been his from before they were married, and he had wanted to throw the old thing out, but they didn't have a lot in the way of furniture nor money being newlyweds, so they had to do with what they had. But Charles had not wanted to move it into their new home, not only because of its weight, but because it was pretty beat up.

Sally had argued with him, saying that they needed it for their clothes, that no one would see it, since it would be in their room anyhow. *"Please Charles, just for the time being. I need somewhere to put our things and we don't have much as it is, so can't we at least keep it just until we're able to afford a new one?"* she had begged.

He almost didn't give in, being a proud man, he wanted to give her the best of everything, but knew that she was right. So, he had given in to her, thinking that just as soon as he could afford to, he would replace it before he'd buy anything else, but Sally had other ideas. She sanded it down, removed all of the drawers and knobs, went down to the local hardware store and bought some varnish and paint for it. In all that time, he didn't know what she was doing, but he thought that he was getting one over on her, because when he finally did cave in, and agree to take it along, it had only made it as far as the garage. He never moved it all the way upstairs, thinking all the while that it would just be a waste of his energy and time, since he was planning on a new one anyhow, but by at least moving it as far as he did, she wouldn't harp on him about it.

She had spent the first few weeks in their new home unpacking everything from the garage, and placing the things where she wanted them to be. With working so hard and late at the garage, he barely noticed how the house looked, the only thing he would have noticed at that particular time was whether or not the bed was there. To this day, he had no idea how she had gotten that big old dresser up the stairs after she had finished her handiwork with it, for she obviously had to have had some help, but she did. She had made it into one of the most beautiful pieces of furniture they owned, even after discarding all of the rest of it and buying all new.

There it stood proudly, as if it were speaking to him, saying, "*See, I'm still here, and you, who wanted to get rid of me. She could see my beauty, but you couldn't see past my scratches and old dull wood! She could though, and she brought it out in me, and now, I'm still here, probably will be after you leave too!*" Charles shook his head and smiled, thinking that he must surely be going nuts to pretend what a "dresser" was saying to him.

She had put love into every corner of this house, making it not only beautiful, but a home. Every time they'd have company over, he'd overhear them commenting on how beautiful their home was and wishing that they could make theirs look as good. He never told Sally of those comments, thinking that it was just *women talk*. In fact, he never really told her what a beautiful job she had done and how proud he was of his home. He had never told her how much warmth she had given it, or how she had a knack for putting things together that, unless someone was as gifted as she, would never even think of putting together.

As he put his elbows onto his knees, he put his head into his hands. "*Oh Sally, I'm so sorry for so many things. I have so many regrets at not telling you how very much you've meant to me, my life, my happiness, my heart. I've never told you so many things that I wish I would have. How I loved to watch you sleeping before I get out of bed to get ready for work, how I loved watching you in the kitchen while you were making dinner, how I loved it when, from out of the blue, you'd walk up and give me a smile and a kiss, then walk away. Or how good it made me feel, watching you try-ing to help Sydney with a homework problem, both of you having the same troubled expressions on your faces, then the glee you both had after figuring it out. How proud I was, every time you walked into the shop, making any man froth at the mouth, at your beauty. How many times they'd ask me, "Who is THAT?," and I'd try to act nonchalant and tell them it was "just my wife," while getting such satisfaction as their eyebrows would rise up and they'd look from you to me and back to you with such a surprised look on their face, that it'd make me want to laugh. I never told you those things. Guess I was always afraid that you'd realize that you'd made a mis-take by marrying me and want someone better. I'm so very sorry, Sally, I'm afraid of messing everything that you've started, up. I'm going to continue to make a lot of mistakes, Sally, so I'm gonna need all the help you can give me.*

Charles punched his pillows a few times to get them com-fortable underneath his head and pulled the blankets over himself. He felt exhausted, but still, sleep eluded him as he lay there staring at the shadows running across the ceiling. Charles woke with a start in the wee hours of the morning; he automatically reached over for Sally, but only finding empti-ness beside him. He glanced at the digital clock sitting on the nightstand by his head, and saw that it was only 4:17 a.m. He didn't remember when he fell asleep, but knew that the last time he checked it was after midnight.

CHAPTER *fifteen*

Charles had finally fallen back to sleep, but it was a restless sleep. He had managed to sleep till almost 7:00 a.m. In the shower, he turned the water on as hot as he could stand it and just stood there while he let it beat into his tired muscles. The first thing he did afterwards was start some coffee, while standing just inside of the refrigerator door, viewing the contents. He was surprised to find that it was pretty well stocked, but then again, Gretta had been doing a lot of those household duties when Sally had become too ill to do them herself and he was too consumed with work and taking care of Sally and Sydney. He pulled out a carton of eggs, and some bacon. He wasn't quite sure on whether to go as far as potatoes, but after deciding that he was going to have to learn, that there was no time like the present, he pulled them out too. The bread took him a little while to locate, as did the pans that he would be using to cook with. After realizing how thin Sydney had become, he wanted to make sure that she was eating enough. Charles found his mood lifting a bit while he was cooking, finding that he kind of enjoyed it.

Sydney had come down from her room that morning, not long after he had. She didn't say much, but seemed to cling to him as she had when she was just a small child. His thoughts suddenly became focused on her needs, and although his ache was still there, he was gratefully distracted from the emptiness that he was feeling in his heart. He welcomed it and not only did he welcome this distraction, but embraced it. Not realizing it, his daughter didn't allow him enough time to become immersed in sadness, nor did it remove the sadness that he was feeling in his life. It alleviated his sadness, as a pain killer alleviates pain without removing it.

He remembered back when he was just a small child, after injuring himself, his mother pleading with the doctor to give him some more pain medication. He remembered the doctor's statement to his mother which at the time he was too young to understand, but remembered the doctor telling his mother, "Although having pain is something that is never pleasant, *it is*, in fact, something that we need to have. For if there is no pain, then there is no injury and we need that pain in order to heal properly. If Charlie continues to take pain medication, I'm afraid that he'll cause himself further harm, because his body won't tell him of his limitations and right now he needs to have limitations in order to heal properly. Otherwise, he could very well spend the rest of his life with even more pain. I won't let that little boy endure an unbearable amount of pain, but nor will I completely remove all of it from him. The reason being is because I don't want to watch him make the pain worse by allowing him to forget that it's there. Trust me, Mrs. Davis; pain is a good thing to have, because as long as we have it, it means that we haven't died. It's there to act as an alarm device to let us know that we need to listen to what information it's giving us and use that information wisely. The human body is quite remarkable. Even though the pain continues, it doesn't mean that we're not healing, it's only a mechanism that allows us to heal without causing ourselves further damage."

Charles poured some juice into a glass for Sydney and setting it before her. He understood how his mother must have felt that day, not wanting to watch him hurt, but knowing unless she allowed him to hurt a little, he wouldn't heal. Somehow, remembering that moment brought more to light than a broken arm. That same concept could be applied to the emotional pain that he and his daughter were feeling at the death of someone, who although played different roles in each of their lives and were missed differently, both felt the loss as deeply and as painfully as the other. In this is where they felt a closeness to one another that wasn't between them before and could not be compared to by anyone else's pain. They seemed to have an unspoken understanding between them that no one else could intrude upon.

Charles wished his daughter would say *something*, rather than just sit there quietly, with such sadness in her face. He wanted to lash out at someone or something for adding this unasked for, unwanted *pain* to his daughter's young life. He, instead, just turned back to his task at hand and started talking about things that wouldn't bring up Sally's death. He found himself dancing around the exact thing he had asked Sydney not to the night before. Meanwhile, he found it quite ridiculous to be doing so, considering the fact that he couldn't remember one time, attempting to make breakfast, or any meal for that matter, on his own, even when Sally was ill from her hysterectomy, did he try to cook. Instead, he'd feed Sydney pop tarts for breakfast or donuts and if she came with him to work back then, he'd always take her to the diner for lunch. Then for dinner, Gretta was usually always there to supply them with at least one nutritious meal.

Where is Gretta, anyhow? I'm surprised that she wasn't already here preparing breakfast before I woke up. When she gets here, I'm sure she's going to feel pretty bad, seeing that I've already done it.

Listen to me, already trying to take advantage of Gretta's generosity. She doesn't owe us anything, but on the other hand, I may have been better off if she wouldn't have taken over so much. Charles thought silently as he glanced towards the back door, as if he wondered if she had knocked and he hadn't heard.

"Dad? Dad?! *Dad!*

"Wha . . . at, Syd?" As smoke curled up from the potatoes in the pan, Charles grabbed a towel to lay over the top of them, while his daughter calmly walked up and shut the burner off, giving him a look that made him feel like the child, rather than the adult.

"That was great thinking kiddo. Guess their done, huh? Good thing that you caught them just in time, one more second and those potatoes probably would've been ruined, huh?" Charles spoke to her retreating back, waiting for the look of disbelief that he knew that she would give him after absorbing his words. *Bingo, gotcha!* Charles happily thought to himself, while watching the desired response appear on his daughter's face, as she turned around to give him a disbelieving look.

"Dad, you just about burnt down the house, trying to cook *and now,* you actually think that I'm going to eat those little pieces of coal? *They're burnt, dad!*"

Sydney's complaining was music to his ears. It gave him a feeling of some *normalcy* that not everything would change, just some things. "How 'bout you do the potatoes from now on? I think that I'm doing about all I can handle, just by trying to make the toast!" Charles tried to look as pathetic as he could, while waiting for another sarcastic response from his daughter.

Instead of getting the response that he expected, Sydney came up to him and gave him a big hug. "Dad, I know you're trying, but do you think that you could try something else? I'm nine and a half years old and I know how to make my own eggs. Besides, I don't even like potatoes in the morning. Mom didn't even make me breakfast in the mornings, she always just gave me cereal. The only one she ever made breakfast for in the mornings was you, dad! So you're the only one that is going to eat those *potatoes that you caught just in time,*" Sydney said with mimicry.

Gretta stood at the kitchen door with her hand raised in a pose that meant that she was just about to knock, when Sydney spotted her and jumped up quickly, almost tripping over her own feet, while yelling at Gretta to come on in at the same time. Though Charles and Sydney were fairing rather well, for their first morning of being left entirely alone, without Sally, Gretta was a welcome sight for sore eyes. She wasn't like all of the well-meaning friends carrying around grief stricken faces, with quiet whispers of disbelief, and shallow promises of *anytime or anything.*

Charles felt relief, as he was sure Sydney felt also, while seeing a smidgeon of brightness seep through the sadness and pain that he knew wasn't going to be just a visitor to them, but would stay and be with them for the remainder of their lives. Even though he knew that it was there to stay, he also knew that before long that same sadness and pain that they were just introduced to, would quickly become familiar. Becoming easier to forget and that even though they weren't invited into their lives, they would be accepted and more tolerable. So he wasn't angry at those who made those promises, knowing that they would never be asked to keep them. He was also aware that they had their own lives, families, and problems to deal with and that he and Sydney would soon fade into the background of their thoughts. He, too, had made those same promises in the past, to others who were going through what he was going through right now, but now he realized how empty those words were. He would never ask anyone for anything, nor would he ever call someone at *anytime*. Not because he didn't think that those who said those words to him were being insincere, but because that's what they felt they needed to say, for whatever reason.

Gretta, thank you for being in our lives. What would I have done without you? You've been not only a life-saver, but have had an enormous impact on all of our lives throughout these years. How different our lives would have turned out if we had never met. I can't remember one single occasion, happy or sad, wonderful or terrible, that you weren't always there. Firm and steady. While never asking for anything in return but always offering more than the others had been willing to give. Everyone should have a "Gretta" in their lives. Charles thought as he felt relief, even if just for a moment, from looking into Sydney's eyes and seeing the pain floating around. It was as if he were looking at the edge of a lake foaming with debris that kept trying to wash it away and leave it on the shore. But the pain in her eyes would be like that dirty foamy filth; it would always be there, lingering, always hanging onto the edge. Clinging to something that refused to let go, but yet at the same time, would be destroyed by keeping it.

"My, my! Would you just look at this kitchen? What's that smell? Charles, you haven't been roasting marshmallows on the stove have you?" as her eyebrows rose up after seeing the charred remains of his endeavor. "Charles, you are going to have the fire department out here, pitching a tent in your front yard, if you plan on cooking three meals a day like this!" Gretta winked at Sydney, as Sydney enjoyed watching her father squirm.

"Come on, Gretta! After all, it was only the potatoes, and besides, you have to give me a little leeway, ladies! I haven't had to do this, ever. So it just might take a time or two, before I get the rhythm to this. Besides, don't I get any credit for trying?

I don't really find eating frozen dinners or having take-out all the time that appealing, do you Sydney?"

"Well, it beats having this yucky smell in the kitchen all of the time. Plus, the food will always taste pretty good and probably won't take quite as long!"

"Now, now, Sydney. I think it's wonderful that your father made this effort this morning *and* other than burning the potatoes, I think that the rest of it looks rather delectable. May I?" Gretta asked Charles without waiting for a reply, as she helped herself to a piece of bacon and a cup of coffee. "Yummy, you cooked this bacon perfectly, it's crispy, *but* it's not burnt. Now how about you give toast a try? I'd like to make myself a little egg and bacon sandwich, of course, if you don't mind me staying for breakfast?" It was more of a statement, rather than a question.

Gretta didn't end up staying long. Charles suspected she wanted to check on how they were fairing and he was grateful to her for that. Not because they wouldn't have survived it, but for the brief reprieve she had given them. He never realized how beneficial small talk could be. He didn't expect everything to be normal right away, or ever, for that matter. Nor did he want to allow things to become very different, as impossible as that was, he felt somewhat in limbo. He knew that he wasn't going to rise out of bed everyday and whip up breakfast, as he tried to do today, but the fear of not knowing what was going to become their own habits, without Sally, was an unbearable thought to grasp. So for now, it gave him a sense of peace to *try* to keep things as she did. Maybe it was his idea of denying that she was gone, for as long as things stayed the same way without her, the less, he felt, that they'd notice her absence.

After Gretta left and breakfast was over, Sydney said that she was going to go back to her room and read for a while. Charles didn't want her to, but he didn't know what else to do.

They were both emotionally drained and even though they had a bit of a break from their sadness that morning, it didn't let them forget this sadness that seemed to penetrate into every thought and action.

"Okay Syd, I'll bet you're still pretty tired anyway. I know that I feel like laying down myself and take a little nap. But if you need me, just holler or find me. I'll be somewhere around here, okay?"

"Sure dad. I will."

She ran up the stairs quickly, as if she couldn't wait to escape from the world into her private, tiny space. Charles couldn't blame her. After all, he could use some time alone, too. He didn't want to even answer the phone or door today, but knew that inevitably someone would feel the need to check up on them. Gretta was the only one he cared about seeing.

Charles tried to lie down for a while and fall asleep, but to no avail. Finally he got up and decided that he'd catch up on some of the bookwork that he wasn't able to find time for while Sally was sick. He really didn't feel like doing it either, but knew that eventually it would have to be done, so decided that he may as well get it over with. Sally was very organized and neat, so it didn't take him long to get familiar as to where she left off. After what seemed like no time at all, Charles finished and much to his dismay, not that much time had passed.

Charles decided that he would need some help. He would have to hire a housekeeper to help with the chores and do the grocery shopping for them. Then he would also have to take Sydney school shopping as her mother had done for her every year. She had grown so much that her clothes seemed to shrink every day.

He also needed to come up with some sort of plan that would work for Randy and him, so that he could be home more with Sydney. He knew that the schedule that he kept before would have to be changed, for he couldn't spend the amount of time that he used to at the shop, with a nine-year-old girl being home alone.

Even though Gretta would make sure she was taken care of, he felt that he would only be taking advantage of her. They had already asked so much of her that he was determined to prove to her that he would be able to handle everything on his own. Charles busied himself on the phone, after looking at the classified section of the newspaper for a responsible house-keeper. After making four appointments to interview them, he figured that he certainly would be able to find one out of four that would be acceptable. After that, he made a mental note to call the paper, so that he could place an ad in it for a secretary and book keeper for the shop. After Charles grew weary of finding ways to pass the time, he went up to Sydney's room to check on her, and after knocking lightly a few times, opened the door to find her in a deep sleep. He pulled the covers over her and lightly kissed her on her forehead, before quietly leaving her room.

He finally succumbed to taking a nap, finding his way to his own room. Once there, Charles rubbed his eyes as he stood up to take off his clothing and crawled into bed left only with his boxer shorts on. He pulled the covers up to his neck and adjusted the pillows, making as little movement as possible. He again remembered that he was alone and didn't have to stay on *his side*. Nor did he have to be careful of waking anyone up by his movements. He looked to his left and felt rather than saw emptiness. *How long will it be, before I'm used to this?* He wondered.

CHAPTER *sixteen*

Jeff, for as long as his young life, didn't have the luxury of having parents that most took for granted. His father was an alcoholic who only became worse. His mother was beaten so much that she, though she was young, began to walk with a hunch and her head always bent to the ground. Their only reprieve from the abuse of his father was when his dad would have a little extra money and was able to stay out drinking later, until after they were asleep. Even those times would become scarcer. He didn't know a world where he could relax and be a child.

It was almost as if he and his mother's roles would reverse during these times. For after his father would beat his mother and then finally pass out, Jeff would be the one who would comfort her, get cold rags for her swollen face, while at the same time telling her that everything would be okay while she would sob onto his shoulders.

Jeff, quite simply, didn't have time to be a child. For various reasons they had to move often. Sometimes it was for lack of rent money, work for his parents, but the most common reason was because of his dad. He didn't like to stay in one place very long. Jeff learned very early in life that his own morality was judged by his parent's behavior, the home he lived in, and the clothes that he wore. This judgment was implacable, causing Jeff's self-imposed isolation.

The consequence of being his friend imposed those same character flaws onto anyone who made that attempt. It was a modern day caste system and he was at the bottom, white trash. He wasn't embarrassed; he had long ago stopped being that, only because he had learned a new way of handling those feelings. He fought. He became the bully, he became the jokester, he became tough, distrustful, angry, and most of all, he became strong. He worked hard at being strong, even though his ten-year-old body would remain as a boy's for a couple more years. All he thought of day and night was getting him and his mother out of the grasp of his father and being safe, somewhere he could never find them. Someday, his father would never lift his hand to his mother, because Jeff was determined to turn the tables on his father.

They lived on the outskirts of town, where the roads were no longer paved. The homes lost their appeal, causing people to move farther away from them. As if by moving farther away from them, they could pretend that they didn't exist. For Jeff, it seemed almost as if they had been quarantined. As if he and his family didn't qualify for the acceptance that others so readily received.

People would look down their noses, with a distasteful look on their face, as if he were a piece of garbage sitting in the middle of their nice cozy lives that they'd just as soon discard than have to figure out how it got there or how they could help. Their expectations of him were always validated, because Jeff found that if he was going to be accused of so many things, without being allowed a defense, he may as well qualify himself.

So these were the cards that were dealt to Jeff that set the stage for his early life. He didn't have time to grumble about the hand that he was dealt because he was too busy simply trying to survive. He was a lonely little nine-year-old boy, with nothing in his young life that made him feel as if he mattered. The only things he had in his life were people that made him feel as if he didn't matter, that he was nothing but a stench in the air, always serving as a constant reminder of his place in a society that didn't want him.

It wasn't until after school one day the following year, when Sydney was walking just ahead of him on the sidewalk and something fell out of her school backpack. He knew that her mother had died that summer before, but didn't know much other than that, other than the fact that he wouldn't know what he would do without his mother around. So he did feel sorry for her *a little.*

She had kept walking without any idea that she had dropped anything. So he reached to the sidewalk to where it landed and picked it up. As he studied it, he felt his insides become warm. It was a picture of her mother and it looked like she was laughing at something really funny. As he turned it over, all it said on the back was *always in your heart, love mom.* As he looked up at her back, with the distance between them becoming farther, he ran after her. He yelled after her to stop for a minute. He could tell that when she heard his voice, it only seemed to make her walk faster.

"Sydney, slow down, will ya? You dropped a picture!" he yelled at her out of breath.

It seemed to take her a moment to realize what he was talking about and as she turned around, she looked at him with those same questioning eyes with the defensive wall up.

As he finally caught up to her, he bent over as if he had been running a marathon, with his hands on his knees taking in gasps of air. He lifted up the hand that held the picture of her mother in response to her questioning look towards him. "Hey, I figured you'd want this back. It fell out of your backpack."

Sydney looked from his eyes to his hand and realized what he was holding. As she slowly retrieved it from his grasp, she looked questioningly at him once again, as if waiting for him to say something snide.

He was used to this look and any other time, would have followed through, but instead he felt a weird feeling in his gut and didn't say a word. He was still panting, but was beginning to catch his breath again.

"Tha . . . thanks, Jeff," was all Sydney could muster out shyly as she uncomfortably shifted her weight from one leg to the other. "Well, I gotta go," Sydney said, as she took a half turn and started on her way.

That was the *icebreaker* for Sydney and Jeff. Even though their lives were very different, they both had more in common than they realized. Neither of them had any brothers or sisters. Sydney had been dealing with sorrow, guilt, and anger since her mother's death. Jeff was carrying the same burdens as Sydney, only his stemmed from the abusive environment that he was living in.

Sydney's classmates were almost afraid to talk to her now that her mother died. Those same classmates shied away from Jeff, because most of them had overheard their parents talking about some escapade that his father did, or they'd whisper about how his dad beat his mother. Jeff didn't seem to be bothered with their attitude as much as Sydney did, but then again, he'd been dealing with those things as far back as he could remember and had gotten used to it. Sydney retreated, where Jeff confronted, but having these experiences somehow became the beginning of a friendship that would last far longer than either one of them dreamed it ever would.

Jeff nonchalantly fell into step with Sydney. Sydney was

about a head taller than Jeff; he was so busy chattering that it didn't seem to faze him. Jeff was somewhat stocky, with dark brown hair and huge brown eyes that looked like two drops of chocolate. He had even succeeded in making Sydney laugh, when he imitated their music teacher. After that, Sydney started loosening up towards Jeff.

He's not so bad, Sydney thought to herself. After reaching the corner in which they would have to go in opposite directions, they bid each other farewell.

CHAPTER *seventeen*

After that afternoon, they started walking home with one another. Even Sydney's only friend Marci would sometimes join them, when she went to Sydney's house after school. Somehow this seemed to open the lines of communication with their classmates and close the distance that they once had with them. Sydney began to come out of her quiet solitude, by becoming friendlier. Jeff, on the other hand, still remained the *tough one*, but even he quit being as aggressive as he used to be and instead replaced it with humor.

They seemed to accentuate each other by bringing the positive points of their individual characteristics to the surface. As mismatched as they were, it became a friendship brought about by the understanding of pain.

In Jeff's ten-year-old mind, he was waiting for the ball to drop, for something to happen to destroy this friendship that he began to have with not only Sydney, but others in his class. He reasoned that the only reason Sydney's dad didn't say anything to her about her friendship with him was due to the fact that he wasn't home enough to realize that he was hanging around. The others in his class were still reluctant to have him into their homes. He knew this was because if they did, their parents wouldn't approve. Jeff wasn't quite as bothered about not being invited into their homes as he was concerned about Sydney's father.

Jeff didn't realize it then, but his worries would soon be faced. One Saturday while they had gone to the park to play some ball with a few of the others, Sydney's father stopped on his way home from the shop. When Sydney spotted him, she went galloping over to where he stood at the edge of the park. The other kids continued playing and shouting their hello's to Sydney's father. Jeff felt that familiar squeeze of his stomach, while he stood there watching Sydney and noticed her motioning for him to come over there. At first he thought he'd just turn his head and act like he hadn't seen her, but knew that wasn't going to work when Sydney and her father started towards him.

"Hey Jeff," she yelled to him as she neared.

He turned his head towards her as if he just now noticed. "Yeah," he yelled back.

"Come here, I want you to meet my dad."

Jeff had a *sink or swim* thought come to his mind and finally, after a moment of debating, thought that he may as well get this over with, knowing in his mind that the *ball was going to drop*, as he forced his legs to move towards them.

Jeff was surprised when instead of getting the look of disdain, followed by the pursed set lips from Sydney's father he instead was greeted with an outstretched hand accompanied by a smile.

"Hello Jeff, I'm Charles, Sydney's father."

"Hi sir," Jeff muttered nervously, dropping his eyes to the ground after his hand was released.

Charles continued, "I'm taking Sydney out for pizza and we thought that maybe you'd like to come along?"

Charles mistook Jeff's moment of hesitation for something else. "I can give you a lift to your house so that you can make sure it's okay with your folks?"

"Uh, no, that's alright. They're not home," Jeff lied. "They probably won't be home till later, anyhow. I . . . I um s'pose I can go, as long as I get home right after."

"I'll tell you what. I have to stop by the house real quick and change. While we're there, maybe you could call them from the house just to make sure, in case they are there? I wouldn't want them to worry, okay?"

Jeff only nodded, feeling the relief of not having Sydney's dad seeing where he lived or the fact that he lied to him about his parents not being home.

At Sydney's house, Jeff was left downstairs to make his phone call. He dialed the familiar number, praying that his father didn't answer. To his relief, his mother answered on the first ring. She seemed a little surprised that he had called her and even more surprised that he was invited somewhere.

"That's fine, Jeff," his mother responded.

The only emotion she had was the surprise at the fact that he had called her at all. Other than that, she didn't ask him when he'd be home or any of the usual questions parents asked their children. In the background, he could hear his father yelling something, but couldn't make out what he was saying. His mother then quickly told Jeff that she had to go and hung up, without even a goodbye. Jeff started worrying, after hanging up the phone, wondering if he should just go home.

Just after Sydney bounced back down the stairs, she told Jeff to come with her next door to tell Gretta that they were ready.

Jeff had met their neighbor several times and thought that she seemed nice. "Is she going with?" Jeff asked while they walked next door.

"Yeah, Gretta always goes with us for pizza on Saturdays. It's her favorite."

Even with the pizza parlor being packed, they didn't have to wait long before getting a table. Jeff noticed a lot of kids from school sitting with their families. Jeff would nod when they'd speak or wave, but feel his stomach knot up when their parents would spot him and lean over and whisper, increasingly afraid that Sydney's father would make this observation too. Jeff had all but forgotten about it by the time the last piece of pizza was being devoured. He was having a good time with Sydney, Gretta, and her dad. Her father seemed pretty funny, making jokes and Gretta always making sure that he was included in all the fun.

It suddenly became blatantly clear to Jeff that his was not the *normal* family lifestyle. He noticed how relaxed Sydney was with her father, something that he had never been able to do with his own. Jeff was used to a lifestyle of staying away from home as much as possible. When Jeff was at home, he was never relaxed around his own father, walking ever so lightly on eggs and inevitably cracking one or two of them no matter how lightly he tread.

Jeff's anxiety level crept back up when Sydney's father informed him that he'd give him a lift home.

"Uh, that's okay; I'll just walk from your house. I don't live very far." Jeff's discomfort was becoming obvious.

"Don't be silly. It's too dark for you to be walking by yourself," Charles replied in a tone that said he wasn't going to argue about it.

Jeff, in his reluctance, had no choice but to tell him in which direction he lived. He knew that this was it. He would no longer be invited to any Saturday night pizzas, let alone even be allowed to hang out with Sydney and all of their new friends. As tough as Jeff tried to be in his young age, the pressures that he was under seemed to swallow him. Jeff sat for a moment, waiting for the *look* from Sydney's dad, before opening the door. It didn't come, much to his astonishment. Instead, Charles turned around, told Jeff how much they enjoyed having him accompany them to dinner and how he hoped that they could do it again. Sliding out of the car quickly, Jeff politely said thanks and took off like a shot to his front door. He quickly slipped inside, closing the door as quickly as he could, as if they would get a glimpse into his *reality* and never return.

Jeff's father was absorbed in watching a show on their small television set that sat on a fold out table in the living room, lifting a can of beer to his lips, without so much as a word to Jeff as he made his way to the back bedroom of the house. Jeff's mother, Margie, stepped out of the bathroom at the same time Jeff was walking down the hallway.

Jeff noticed that she had been crying again, along with some fresh bruises on her arms.

"Oh, hi honey, did you just get home?" Margie asked somewhat distantly.

"Yeah mom."

His mother only nodded, before quietly going into her own bedroom and closing the door softly. No hug, no kiss, no questions, it was just as if he were some kind of nonentity. Jeff's anger began building. Normally his anger was directed towards his father, but on this night, he felt it building towards his mother also. As he lay down on his stomach on the bed, he reviewed the events of the evening and wished for the very first time that he had never been born. He was a tired little boy, with a mother that was too deeply absorbed in her own pain that that was all that mattered to her and a father who simply knew no other feeling other than hatred. He felt a small tear make it out of the corner of his eye, as he laid his head into his folded arms.

It was as if an alarm went off in Jeff's young ten-year-old mind. He felt like a piece of garbage being thrown away, day after day, until the one day would come when he would simply disappear. His mother always told him that she could never make it on her own with a ten-year-old to take care of. By saying this to Jeff, he, instead, heard that if she were alone and without him, she could leave. Instead, since he was here, he was not only the reason for her abuse, but also the reason she couldn't escape from it. So he was forced to watch his mother sacrifice herself to this abuse, because of him and for this his anger grew.

He was too young to realize that it wasn't his fault; that the way his father treated them was wrong. There had been a few times when his dad was beating his mother and Jeff tried to stop him. His dad had hit him so hard that the very air was knocked out of his small body. His mother's screams would always be silenced with another slap. His mother would continually tell Jeff not to tell anyone, to keep it a secret, which only furthered the shame that he carried with him. He was unable to free the heaviness in his heart. If he were to tell anyone, then he would be responsible for causing his mother further harm and hadn't he already caused so much of it just by being the anchor that held her captive?

So with these thoughts leaving Jeff angry, anxious, and hurt, Jeff fell asleep on top of the bed. No one came in to check on him, give him a hug good night, or make sure that he was covered up and safe. Jeff was all alone.

The next morning, Jeff awoke to the burst of sunlight flooding through the thin faded sheet that served as a curtain. He was still dressed in the clothes that he had worn the day before, as he made his way to the bathroom. He walked quickly back to his room and changed into another pair of faded, worn jeans, while pulling a tee shirt out of one of his drawers. After lacing his tennis shoes up, he didn't wake either of his parents up. They too, were left where he had found them when he came home. His mother, probably still sleeping in their bedroom and his dad moved from the chair, to the couch, snoring loudly. On the old coffee table were the remnants of his father's night. Empty beer cans littered the top of the coffee table, along with an over flowing ashtray. One cigarette butt didn't quite make it to the ashtray and lay there adding yet another burn mark to the coffee table. Jeff walked as lightly as he could through the living room, to avoid waking his father. As he almost reached the door, his dad readjusted himself on the couch, causing Jeff to tense up. Jeff waited to move until again he heard his dad resume snoring. He opened the thin door as quietly as it would allow, while pushing the screen door open.

It was quiet and still this early hour of the morning, the only noise breaking the silence was a dog barking in the distance. Jeff headed towards town, not knowing what he would do once he got there. Jeff got to the end of the dirt road and decided that he'd take the familiar route to Sydney's house. He walked slowly down the street, wishing that he had grabbed a piece of bread or something to fill his rumbling tummy.

He was nearing Sydney's home, looking for a sign of movement. He was concentrating so hard on Sydney's home, that he didn't notice Gretta watering her plants on her front porch. Gretta watched him for a moment and then started down her steps.

"Jeff? Why it is! What brings you out at this early hour?"

Both Gretta and Charles were aware of the things that took place in Jeff's home. Charles had confided to Gretta that he was skeptical about letting Sydney spend so much time with Jeff, because of the horrible rumors he had heard around town about his father. Gretta had set Charles straight, saying that was even more reason to let her hang around with Jeff.

She expressed her displeasure with Charles openly, saying that he was no better than the other's who spread those rumors. She told him that he should be more concerned as to how to help this young boy, rather than sweep him under the carpet as so many have already done. Her reasoning was because Jeff had already had so much in his young life, that to allow him to have a friendship with Sydney would help to build his confidence, rather than affirm what others were saying. She had told Charles that by elevating their expectations of Jeff, he would in turn strive to achieve them. Gretta's sight was so much more objective than others. Gretta was never intrusive to anyone and she treated Jeff with the same regard. She didn't want to push him into talking about anything that he wasn't ready to. Instead, Gretta would just wait patiently, while continuing to be kind.

Jeff had been caught off guard. He thought about fibbing to Gretta, telling her that his mom had asked him to run to town for something, but then he was afraid that she'd volunteer to drive him there and he had no money. So after a brief hesitation, he settled on the truth.

"I just felt like walkin is all."

Gretta studied him briefly and dove in head first. "It's a good thing, too, because you know what I just pulled out of the oven? I'll bet they're cool enough, too, by now. It's delicious, warm, chewy, glazed cinnamon rolls! What d'ya think, you do like them don't you?"

Jeff thought of his rumbling tummy and the rumbling won. "Um, yeah, guess so."

"Well then, come on!" Gretta led him through the front door and into the back of her home which was the kitchen, poured a big glass of milk for Jeff and placed a large cinnamon roll on a napkin in front of him.

Gretta rested her chin on her fist, "So? Is it good or not?"

Jeff took a quick breath in between bites, "The best I've ever had!"

After Jeff took the last swallow of milk, he noticed Gretta look to the clock, then back to Jeff. "Listen Jeff, I know that Sydney and her dad are probably starting to move around now, because church starts at 10:00. Would you like to go with us today?"

"I, I uh, don't have any other clothes to wear."

Gretta smiled, "What's wrong with what you got on? God doesn't mind what you're wearing, he's just glad when you come to church."

Jeff had never been to church before in his life and didn't know what to expect, but thinking it would probably be better than going back home, he agreed to go. The only thing he knew about church was from the television.

"It's settled then. Listen, I've got to go take my robe off and put some clothes on, why don't you go make yourself comfortable in the living room. If you want some more cinnamon rolls, help yourself, the milk's in the fridge. Okay? One more thing, why don't you call home and let your folks know, so that they won't worry about you? The phone is hanging on the wall in the kitchen."

Jeff smiled and nodded. Jeff stopped in the short hallway that led from the kitchen to the living room and glanced at some pictures Gretta had hanging. He studied each picture, wondering what they were thinking right then, as they all wore huge smiles. Jeff wasn't going to call home this time, because he figured that it was probably his phone call last night that had caused his mom her new bruises. As he heard Gretta moving around upstairs, he lifted the receiver and acted like he was calling, just in case she was listening. After hanging the receiver up, he walked into the living room and looked around at how nice everything was.

Gretta came back all dressed and ready to go, with two Bibles in her hands. "Here you go Jeff. You can keep this one. I always keep an extra one around, just in case."

Jeff looked down at the Bible; it was black with a zipper that went all the way around it. He mumbled a quick thank you, as he clutched his new Bible.

Gretta sat down on the couch, while patting the empty spot next to her for him to sit down. "Have you ever read a Bible before?" Jeff shook his head. "While we wait for Sydney and Charles to call, I'll show you a couple of things that will help you." As she opened his Bible, she pointed out how he could find a Bible verse and explained why some of it was printed with red ink. "I'm sorry we don't have more time, but that might help you a little bit, huh?"

The phone rang at Gretta's house and after quickly telling Charles that Jeff would be joining them this morning for church, Jeff felt the familiar knots in his stomach. He started having doubts about whether he should be going. He was suddenly frightened.

"You ready, sport?" Gretta asked with a smile and a soft pat on his back.

Sydney was standing by the door of her father's car, when Gretta and Jeff walked up. Sydney, after firing a multitude of questions at Jeff, seemed to finally be satisfied with his answers by the time they reached the church parking lot.

Jeff was unfamiliar and tried to exhibit as little nervousness as possible in front of the others in Sunday school class, some of them being his classmates. The teacher began and Jeff was hooked. Some of the others in the class acted bored, but Jeff hung on every single word. His heart needed nourishment as his stomach had earlier that morning. After Sunday school was over, Sydney brought him back upstairs for the church service. Jeff watched everyone sing songs that he had never heard before. He noticed some crying and raising their hands. After they had been seated, the pastor began and all was quiet throughout the entire service with the exception of an Amen or Praise God.

After the church service was over, everyone milled around, chattering, and shaking hands. While Jeff was quietly standing in the doorway, waiting on Sydney, Gretta, and her father, he felt a hand touch his shoulder. Startled, he turned to see the Pastor smiling at him with kind eyes.

"Hello there, young man. I don't think that I've seen you here before?"

Mustering up as much politeness as he could, Jeff spoke. "Uh, well um, no sir, this is my first time."

The Pastor stuck his hand out towards Jeff. "I'm Pastor Williams and you are?"

"Jeff."

"Well Jeff, I certainly hope you'll visit us again. It was nice to have you." After the Pastor had walked away to talk with some of the other parishioners, other's came up to Jeff and introduced themselves to him also. Jeff felt welcome in a world he thought no longer welcomed him.

That early spring Sunday was the beginning of hope for Jeff. He didn't want to leave the confines of this kindness that felt as if he were sitting in front of a nice warm fire on a frigid cold winter's night. As the parishioners started thinning out, Jeff again experienced a loneliness more profound than he ever had before, after he realized that now he would have to step back into the darkness called home.

Charles was pulling out of the church parking lot when he brought Jeff out of his reverie. "Jeff, you're coming over to have Sunday dinner with us, aren't you? Gretta and I switch off every Sunday, and this is my Sunday. Well, that is if you want to risk it or not?" Charles chuckled with the girls, all of them knowing that even though it was *his* Sunday to cook, that Gretta took care of the bulk of the cooking. Charles had a lot of good points, but cooking wasn't one of them.

Jeff felt the dark cloud hanging over his head, start to fade away again. "Uh, sure, I guess," not wanting to sound too eager.

"Dad always grills on the BBQ when he's gotta cook, cause otherwise he tries to burn the house down," Sydney explained to Jeff.

Randy and Becky joined them that Sunday afternoon. After they had all eaten, Randy and Charles pulled a badminton set out of the garage and set it up. Becky and Gretta sat on the lawn watching and rooting for Sydney and Jeff.

Jeff couldn't remember ever having so much fun. The dread of having to go home was approaching swiftly. After helping Gretta straighten up Charles kitchen, Becky and Randy offered to give Jeff a ride home. Jeff declined resolutely, knowing that with it still being sunny out, they wouldn't argue. He waited until after he was sure Becky and Randy's car turned the corner and they were out of sight, before saying his goodbyes to the rest of the group. He picked his Bible up from the picnic table and started home.

CHAPTER *eighteen*

Jeff wandered home slowly, while studying the outside of his new Bible thinking about the stuff his Sunday school teacher had said. She talked about praying and said that God hears you no matter where you are. She said that when you prayed, just to act like you were talking to one of your friends. So as Jeff walked home, he thought he'd try it, as he said a silent prayer. As he neared his home, relief flooded through him at the realization that his dad's truck was not in the driveway.

"Mom, mom, I'm home?" Jeff didn't hear a response. He walked towards the back of the house where the bedrooms were and heard his mother's soft sobbing coming from hers.

Apprehensively, Jeff pushed her door ajar. After peeking inside, he found his mother on the edge of her bed on her side, with her back facing him. Jeff quietly walked around the bed, as he lowered himself to a squatting position beside her. She lay there, almost like a child, while Jeff pushed her hair off of her forehead, seeing yet more bruises decorating her face, a swollen lip, along with her eye also swollen almost shut.

"H . . . h . . . he's n . . . not coming back. H . . . he's ta . . . taken his clo . . . clothes and all of the money that we had."

Margie hiccupped as she hugged Jeff to her. "W . . . wh . . . what are we going to do?"

"How do you know he won't be back, Mom?" Jeff was glad, but he knew that he shouldn't be feeling so happy when his mom was so sad.

"Cause, he was packing before I got up this morning and said that he couldn't stand being around us anymore. Th . . . that he had someone else and that they had been planning on leaving together long before now. H . . . he said that he couldn't stand the sight of me and that we were just dead weight to him." She wiped her dripping nose with her hand and started to sob uncontrollably again. "I kept begging him to stay and he just kept hitting me and telling me to get away from him."

Jeff just let her hang on to him, not liking the palpitating of his heart. The words "dead weight" kept hurtling through his head. A hurt like he had never known before swept through him. His mother didn't realize the impact of her words on him. Not only did she validate the fact that his own father couldn't stand him, but that she, too, didn't love him enough to be happy that someone who didn't was gone. The renewed sense of self that Jeff had earlier, slipped through his fingers quickly, as if he were trying to carry water with his palms. Worthlessness came back at him, as if someone were throwing a brick right through his heart. She had said that he took everything, yes, indeed he had. Jeff had not only hit poverty level on a financial level, as he was used to, but on an emotional level also.

An uncontrollable rage gripped Jeff so strongly that he pushed his mother away and screamed that he hated her, too, as he ran out of the bedroom, out of the house, and didn't stop until he could no longer run. Jeff had run the opposite way from town, towards the woods. Once there, Jeff began crying, trying to push the tears back inside as he angrily brushed them away. He didn't know how long it had been that he sat there, but by the time he decided to walk back, it was dark, with it even darker in his heart.

In the distance he saw a car's headlight's coming down the road slowly. He stepped to the side of the road as he saw the car slowing down as it neared him. With the headlights blinding him, he heard a voice say his name, but couldn't place it. Jeff kept walking, trying to look tough. A figure got out of the car and Jeff was now close enough to make out the tall lanky figure of Randy.

"Jeff? It's me, Randy. Thank God you are okay! We've been looking all over for you for a couple of hours now. Your mother called Sydney's house and told us what had happened. She's been very worried about you. We've all been worried about you, Jeff."

"What's my ma so worried for?" Jeff was unable to hide the anger in his voice.

"She loves you and she didn't know where you went."

Jeff was silent.

"Listen, why don't you get in the car and we can talk about this on the way back to your house. I've got to let everyone know that you're alright. You know that we all care about you a great deal, Jeff, and all we want to do is help you."

"I don't need your help."

Randy added sternness to his voice. "I didn't ask if you needed it or not, Jeff, 'cause I'm offering it to you whether you want to accept it or not. You can't push me away, 'cause I'm not going away, ever. Do you understand what that means? Well, let me tell you anyhow. It means that I care about what happens to you and with saying that, when something bad happens to you, I'm going to help you to make it better."

While Randy stood there, he understood the pain that Jeff was feeling. Jeff's mother explained what had happened, in between her sobs. Becky stayed at the house with Jeff's mother, attending to her injuries, in case Jeff came back there. Gretta stayed with Sydney at Sydney's house while Charles and Randy went looking for him. If Randy hadn't come across him when he did, they would have had to call the police. Becky wanted to make a police report anyhow, for the injuries that Margie had sustained, but the mere suggestion only antagonized Margie more. So Becky dropped it, for the time being. Becky worked at the shelter for abused women and children, so she was well informed as how to handle situations delicately.

Jeff reluctantly got into the front seat of Randy's car and Randy turned around in the middle of the road. As soon as they returned to Jeff's home, Randy called Gretta over at Sydney's house and informed her that Jeff had been found, as well as okay. Gretta told him that she would let Charles know when he checked back in at the house.

Randy offered to take Margie and Jeff to their house for the night, but Margie, with her almost clownish fat lip, refused. Becky nodded at Randy to leave them alone.

On their drive home, Becky mentioned that she felt somehow that they would be alright. Randy wished he had as much confidence as Becky did. That night he and Becky prayed together for Jeff and his mother, not realizing that God had already taken action. He was preparing a route for them that was difficult for others to see or understand. In their prayer's they spoke from their hearts, knowing that God had his own way of doing things in his infinite wisdom.

That day turned both Jeff and Margie's life around. Comparatively, it was a loss they had suffered as Charles and Sydney had when her mother died. There were more similarities than differences, they all went through a grieving process, they all had pain to work through, but more importantly it caused Margie and Jeff to reach out to other's as Charles and Sydney had had to do.

Although it had been an unhealthy, abusive relationship that they had, it was still painful. Becky had talked Margie into seeking counseling at her shelter for both she and her son. Margie began seeing the same things in a new way. She developed patterns for herself that someday would become good habits, while gaining strength emotionally and physically. In doing so, Jeff, too, became more optimistic and emotionally stronger. This door that opened for them was treated more like an emergency exit out of their old lives. They escaped as quickly as the time it took their wounds to be healed, leaving behind memories that would fade, as would the scars left on their hearts.

Margie didn't turn around quite as quickly as other's had hoped she would. She still had times that she would have welcomed her old environment back with open arms to escape the terrifying one that she was left to face alone. Becky and she had bumped heads on more than one occasion. Becky's was from the frustration she felt some days, when Margie seemed to be going backwards, rather than forwards. Margie's was more from the unknown and having her role as a victim being pulled away.

Becky expected this to happen. She knew that the environment that most of these women fled, were often the environment that they found themselves falling back into quickly, because it was all they knew or felt deserving of. She knew that if they didn't allow themselves the time it took for them to gain strength emotionally, the more susceptible they would become to the same type of predator that they had left. For as much time as it took them to become so defeated, often would take as much time to repair. That is why Becky pushed so hard in the beginning, first helping Margie find a job to get her on her feet and give her some independence, without having to rely on anyone for her basic needs. Then she helped her to find the little house in town that she could feel was her own and away from some of the memories of the old one. Becky also wanted her out of the old house just in case he decided to come back. The counseling was a very important issue for Becky. When Margie would start sinking again, it was usually when she failed to show up for her session. Slowly though, one by one, Becky was removing each control that her husband had had over her life.

The process was long and arduous to rebuilding Margie's psyche. She needed constant reassurance, support, and positive input in her life, so that when one small thing went wrong in her life, it was given less and less attention. There were days when Margie just wanted to throw her hands into the air and give up. Her sessions with the counselor were difficult for her, some days she felt worse leaving than she had when she walked in. It was as if she were removing thorns out of her heart, reliving, retelling, and revealing her shame and guilt. It was hard for Margie to understand that by exposing all of her secrets that she had buried for so long, how it was going to improve her life. Walking slowly through her pain was for her far more difficult than just simply pretending that it wasn't there. Gradually, Margie was starting to show signs of improvement. Physically, she started taking pride in how she looked when she left the house for work in the mornings. Mentally, she was starting to deal with disappointments that in the past would leave her in bed for days, and instead, shrug her shoulders, not giving them the control that she used to in the past. Spiritually, she was finally given hope. It was through learning about God's obsessive love for her that brought all of these things together. She finally realized what it felt like to really and truly *matter*.

Margie found a job as a receptionist in a local attorney's office, answering the phones and doing some light secretarial work. With that job, she was able to afford to move them into a tiny home in town. It wasn't much, but it was cozy and enough room for the both of them to have their own breathing space. Although by the time Jeff had reached his teens, she hardly ever saw her son. He had gotten a job at the shop with Charles and Randy after school and on Saturdays. He played a lot of baseball and worked hard at getting perfect grades. He knew that he would need those grades to be able to get a scholarship for college. He had begun fighting for the dreams that he wanted to achieve some day.

Although Jeff and his mother had come a very long way, they still had miles and miles to go. They still had their bad days, but in comparison, their days would never be as bad as they once were. They found they enjoyed being able to speak their minds, without fear of retribution. This, for them, was the confidence that they had needed so desperately in the past.

They had found through their suffering a whole new world and the ability to be grateful for it. It was something that they wouldn't have been able to understand without having that agony in their lives. They found that they would not have to trudge through life on their own anymore. They both found a circle in which they could belong, where people accepted them with all of their wounds, failures, and baggage, with open arms and love.

CHAPTER *nineteen*

Sydney, on the other hand, was just as involved as Jeff was, but lacked the drive that he had. She didn't have the same concern as to how she would pay for college as he did. Nonetheless, she was well aware that she would have to maintain decent grades to even get into one, so to that degree she worked hard. Sydney joined the track team and found her own part time job at the grocery store. She also found some trouble to get into every once in a while, but always straightened up when push came to shove.

Even with their busy schedules, Sydney and Jeff remained steadfast and loyal friends. Their circles had widened, with Becky, Randy, Gretta, Charles, and Margie. They both gained confidence as the years passed through high school, after realizing that the storms that they had gone through made them both stronger. Their strengths at that early age, varied.

Jeff found a hunger for God's love. He found he could make a difference in the world that others couldn't. He had the compassion and firsthand knowledge of what it was like to go through life without love. So he became a fighter in a different way; he fought for himself and others that needed the kind of understanding that only he could give. He would no longer be ignored as if he didn't exist.

Sydney didn't see God in the light that Jeff did. She took Him for granted at times. She didn't have the same hunger that Jeff had for Him. Instead, she placed her strength in the anger that she felt towards Him, wanting to retaliate in any way she could. So she ignored his presence in her life, turning away and running as fast and furious in the other direction that she could.

Jeff and his mother still attended church every Sunday, Jeff still carrying that same black Bible that Gretta had given to him when he was ten, only now the zipper was broken. Margie also had her own. On her first day, while sitting in the counselor's office waiting to be seen, a woman walked up to her and handed her a Bible. All she said was, "I thought maybe you'd like to have this, it's pretty good reading." Margie opened it up and in the front page of the Bible was a handwritten note.

It read, *God knows what you are going through, for that is why you are here. God listens to your thoughts, for that is why you are here. God feels the pain you are feeling in your heart, for that is why you are here. God Loves you, for that is why you are here. God knows your fear, for that is why you are here. No matter what you have done, are doing, or will do, God loves you, no matter what! Open your heart, let him inside, and he will take you places you've never ever imagined going. Love, Someone who knows*

When Margie had finished reading it, she felt goosebumps rising up and down her arms as she turned around quickly, but the woman had gone. Margie would never forget that day. As she waited to get into the counselor's office, she opened it slowly, caressing the pages as she looked down to the words. She read and reread the note so many times that she knew it by heart. Margie did open her heart, and in doing so, found a love so encompassing and complete that she couldn't imagine spending even one more day without it.

This was how Margie found such a close friendship in Gretta. Gretta had hit her early seventies and noticeably so, although it didn't come about clamorously. It began in diminutive ways, such as tiring rapidly, spending less time out in her garden as she used to, and seeming to become more and more forgetful. Even the bounce in her step seemed to diminish.

One morning, Margie had arrived at Gretta's home, armed with a box of donuts. Gretta was still in her bathrobe as she answered the door to greet her. Margie immediately noticed that Gretta was talking with a slur in her speech, as if forming the words had become difficult. An alarm went off in Margie's head as she called Charles at the shop. Margie didn't yet own a car, so Charles took Gretta to the hospital, with Margie sitting in the back seat. Once they arrived, Gretta was taken back to one of the emergency rooms. Margie was worried sick about her friend, as was Charles.

Charles noticed the concern on Margie's face. "She'll be alright, Margie. Gretta's a tough old bird."

Charles was saying it more for his own benefit, than for Margie's. He knew that something was definitely not right with Gretta's speech. She had been like his mother and carried both he and Sydney through many tough patches. When the doctor came out, he confirmed Charles worst fears. Gretta had had a minor stroke while she slept and that's what caused her speech to become impaired. Charles and Margie were both allowed to see her, before leaving.

Before leaving the hospital, Charles told the doctor that he'd call her children to let them know what had happened. Margie and Charles were quiet on the way home from the hospital, both lost in their own thoughts.

"Margie, are you okay?" Charles asked her as he pulled into her driveway.

She only nodded as she reached for the car door handle and got out.

Charles went home to call Gretta's boys up. Her son's, of course, were devastated and agreed that they would make arrangements to get there within hours. Charles was crushed after speaking to each one of them on the phone. The doctor said that they would only need to keep her there for a day or two, since the stroke was such a minor one, but the implication of her having another one that was more severe and causing even more damage hung in the air as the doctor walked away.

Charles met with Gretta's sons and after a long discussion of trying to convince them that he could take care of her, they decided that after she was released from the hospital that she would go home with them. The oldest one would be the one to care for her. He convinced Charles that they had more resources for medical care where they lived than they had in the small town that Gretta lived. So after packing most of her things up from the house, Sydney and Charles said their tearful goodbye's to Gretta and her family, feeling as if another chapter of their lives was closing.

PRESENTLY

CHAPTER *twenty*

Sydney was jerked out of her misery from the sound of the doorbell. As she looked at her watch she thought to herself, *surely Becky isn't already here?* She slowly straightened up and slipped quickly into the bathroom to splash some cold water on her face. After Sydney looked in the mirror and found that her mask was again in place, she made her way down the staircase as the doorbell rang again.

Sydney opened the door, with as much of a smile as she could muster and found herself face to face with Margie. "Margie! How are you?" as Margie and Sydney hugged each other.

"I'm sorry; I probably should have called first."

"Don't be ridiculous, you know that you don't have to call!" Sydney replied as she noted Margie taking in her appearance. "I . . . I'm just sorry that you have to see me looking this way. I just, well, decided to wait on getting a shower in this morning, since I would be packing all day anyhow, but now I am regretting my decision."

Margie noticed the tone in Sydney's voice sounding *too happy*. So Margie decided to dive head first into why she was here, something that she didn't do often, but had learned that it was the best way. She had learned through the years that it was always best to remove an obstacle right away. That way it wouldn't be allowed to become so cumbersome that it couldn't be moved. After they had gotten the initial formalities out of the way, Margie spoke first. Taking off her wet jacket, they made themselves comfortable at the kitchen table with a steaming cup of coffee in front of them.

"Sydney, again I'm sorry that I popped in here unannounced, but I thought that I was probably the last person that you'd want to see right now. You see, I've talked to Jeff, he . . . well, he's worried about you. He has been for a while." Margie noticed a flash of betrayal cross Sydney's face quickly and then just as quickly vanish. "Sydney, I have made it a point not to get involved with you and Jeff's relationship. God knows I've not handled mine very well."

Margie's eye's then filled up. "Sydney, I know what dreadful pain you are dealing with right now. First, losing your father and then losing a child. It's more than even I can begin to imagine. When I received the phone call that my only and first grandchild had been taken, you have no idea the anger and sadness I had towards God. I asked myself why would this great God, who's taken us so far, drop us into this vast, horrible place, and leave us here to lick our wounds. You are my daughter, Jeff is my son and it is such torture for me to see you both go through this." Sydney stayed silent, still simmering from the fact that Jeff called his mother and told her of their problems.

Margie continued, "I don't have the answers, I don't have the cure for your pain, I don't know the reasons, but I do know that I trust and believe that God does. Back when I was with Jeff's father, even as hateful and mean as he treated me, I clung to him. Why I clung to him was because I didn't have anything else to cling to. It's as if I see a stranger when I look at where I used to be in my life. When he finally left me, I felt as if I was dying a slow death, even though the abuse would finally end. That's because I was being left with nothing to cling to, only myself. I caused Jeff a lot of hurt and pain, because I wasn't able to cope, to see the light, so to speak. I was so encrusted with darkness in my life that to come out of that darkness and into the light, it would hurt my eyes that were so accustomed to that very darkness. Customarily, that's how a lot of us would rather live our lives. In the dark, fumbling around, stubbing our toes often, rather than face the pain for a moment and see the wonders before us that we had been missing while in the dark." Margie paused.

"I guess what I'm saying, Sydney, is that both you and Jeff have been walking in the dark and are starting to get used to it again. Sometimes the way out of our own pain is to visit someone else's. Then we forget about our own, and it loses some of its *zip*. You both have devised this wall between each other that you can't see the pain in one another anymore. You've both imprisoned yourselves in a solitary confinement, leaving yourselves nothing to cling to, but your own individual pain. As I told you before, I don't understand many of the tragedies that God bestows upon us, but I do know that when we have an unwavering faith in Him and hand it over, He gives us triumph. I've found that life is a lot like school, the more we study, the more we learn, then the better we become because of it." Margie then reached down deep inside of her oversized bag for the Bible that was given to her. Margie explained the story of how she received the Bible and then read Sydney the note inside that was weathered from being read over so much.

Sydney stood up with her coffee cup and went to pour herself some more, giving herself a moment to regain her composure. Margie stayed silent, praying a silent prayer, while hoping she didn't push too hard. Margie watched Sydney's thin body standing with her back turned to her, as Sydney let the floodgates once again open. Margie stood up and went to Sydney, hugging her to her as Gretta had done for Sally so many years ago.

"I'm so sick and tired of losing everything in my life that I love! I want it all back, Margie!" Sydney cried.

Margie gently pushed Sydney back to where she could look into her eyes. "I remember when, in one of my very first counseling sessions, I remember saying something similar to the counselor. She then asked me a question. She had asked me if I would, if given the chance, have erased getting married to Jeff's father, being pregnant with Jeff, so that my life wouldn't have turned out so horribly. She didn't ask me if I could erase only one of those things, but all of them. She told me the reason being that if I didn't have even one of those things that it would have upset the others that followed. My answer was no; that I would not have erased any of those things that happened, because then I wouldn't have had my son Jeff or have arrived as to where I'm at now in my life. So my question to you, Sydney, is that if you could take back ever having Jacob be born if you would have known ahead of time that you would only have him for those four short years, would you?" Sydney shook her head no.

"Of course you wouldn't, because even though you only had him in your life for that brief period, he awakened a love inside of you that you never knew could exist. None of us want to erase that. Think only of how much Jacob gave to your life in that short time, rather than how much you have lost and then you will see that there is no comparison. You and Jeff have had a life filled with many ups and downs. He needs you in his life and you need him; are you now going to give up and erase it, too? Are you going to keep punishing yourselves by not only losing your son, but each other in the process?

"Sydney, you have had an insurmountable amount of sadness in your young life, but look at how you've been blessed. Take the focus off of the pain for a while and think about all of the blessings that you've been given. Without having some pain in your life, you can never know joy. God has a way of shrinking that pain up, rolling it into a ball, and throwing it right out of the ball park, but first, you have to let him have it."

"I don't think I left a lot of hope between Jeff and me. In fact, I was thinking about not going back at all," Sydney quietly stated as she stared at the floor.

"Sydney, I will support you in whatever you choose to do. This is for you and Jeff to figure out. I love the both of you and would love to see you both fix the damage in your marriage, but that's what *I* want. Just promise me that you will sit down with Jeff and talk about this, face to face, before deciding anything, whether it be staying together or parting ways. Okay?"

Sydney's eyes were swollen and red as she looked sadly to her mother-in-law. "I promise."

Sydney walked Margie to the door. Margie was sliding her arms into her jacket and then she quickly hugged Sydney and whispered. "Sydney, talk to God, tell him where you hurt. He will see to it that it is removed, I promise. You must let Him take it; don't clutch it so tightly that He can't remove it from your life. I'm praying for you Sydney and I'm praying for Jeff. I love you dearly, always know that. If you need anything, please call me. I'm not here to take sides, Sydney. I'm here because I know that without others, it gets pretty tough to stand on my own two feet. I love you." Sydney watched her walk quickly to her car with the rain continuing to fall steadily.

CHAPTER *twenty one*

Jeff announced to his secretary that he was leaving for the day, as he held onto his briefcase and the other arm filled with more paperwork. He was tired of pouring over cases that all seemed to blur together. He thought that somehow he would be relieved when Sydney left, but now that she had been gone for four days, he found himself missing her. Not missing the woman that left, but the woman that used to occupy their home, his life, and his heart. He spent hours in his home, thinking, praying and even picking up the black Bible that he had been neglecting for so long. He continued to reminisce by looking at their countless photo albums.

By the third day without her, he finally got down on his knees by his bed and had a heart to heart talk with God. He very rarely included the formality of actually getting down on his knees, but he was going to beg this time. He begged God for help. Help to save his marriage, help repair his own heart, help to understand his wife, and most of all, help to just get through another day. So on this fourth day while he sat at his desk, unable to concentrate on the file in front of him, he made the decision to take a break. It was only ten o'clock in the morning, but he was already exhausted.

After arriving at home, he went straight to the phone. Jeff glanced at his watch and thought of the two hour difference in time, deciding it was okay to go ahead and call his mother. He hadn't talked to her much since Jacob's death, keeping their conversations short. He would always assure her that everything was fine, still being the protective son. This time, though, he needed *her*. He was the one that needed the reassurances, someone to take over and tell him *that everything would be okay*. So he slowly picked up the phone and dialed the familiar number.

Jeff sat in the chair, with the phone up to his ear, as he listened to it ring. It rang several times and just as he started to hang the phone up, he heard the familiar voice on the other end answer. Jeff's throat started to close as he choked out in a voice that didn't feel like his own. "Hi mom, it's Jeff."

"Why Jeff, what a surprise this is! How are you doing?"

"Jeff? Jeff, are you there?"

In a strangled voice, "Yeah, I'm here mom. Listen, I . . . I um need to talk to you, do you have the time?"

Margie sensed that Jeff was crying, through his voice on the other end of the phone. "Of course, I have time. What's the matter, Jeff?"

Margie listened to Jeff unload his heart. She heard what he was saying and even heard the things that he hadn't said. Margie and Jeff talked for over an hour on the phone. When Margie hung up the phone, she felt confident that Jeff seemed comforted after being able to open up and talk with someone about all that he was going through. She called the attorney she had worked with throughout the years and asked him if it would be okay if she didn't come into work today. Margie knew it would be, because she suspected that he only continued to keep his practice open to give her a job. He was almost retired, doing small cases, advising and such, so her work load was always light these days. They had a relationship that was more of a friendship, as opposed to an employer's relationship with an employee.

Margie then spent her morning fussing around her tiny house, while deciding how she could help. After praying, she came to a decision. That's when she had decided to drive over to Sydney's home.

CHAPTER *twenty two*

Sydney went back to packing with a vengeance after Margie left. *Did Margie say that Jeff called her and told her that he still loves me? Did I hear her right? Does he still think that we can fix this? I did promise her that I would sit down with Jeff face to face and talk, before deciding to end our marriage.* The thoughts were all flying around inside of Sydney's head, taking turns as they landed. Sydney was feeling a slight lift in her mood, although still reluctant to give up her clutch on her pain and anger. A glimmer of hope as small as the eye of a needle, sparkled just enough in her heart to catch her eye.

Sydney accomplished more in those couple of hours than she had ever dreamed she would. She was so consumed with her thoughts and her packing, that she almost didn't notice the doorbell. *Oh my gosh, Becky must be here.* Sydney started down the stairs, while yelling for Becky to come on in.

Becky walked in like the ray of sunshine hidden behind a dark cloud. Sydney met her at the bottom of the stairway, as they hugged each other tightly. Sydney let go and looked at Becky's always smiling freckled face. Becky's hair was straight, shoulder length, and fire engine red. She was only five feet two inches, with muscular legs and a thin waist. Her eyes were a light blue that sparkled as the brightest star in the sky. She and Randy made a cute couple, with his tall lanky height next to Becky's short petite body.

"It's so good to see you, Sydney!" Becky's eyes gave Sydney the once over. "You are far too skinny though; doesn't that husband of yours make enough money to feed you?"

Sydney just laughed, not wanting to destroy the happiness that was in her heart for a fleeting moment. "You will never change, Becky. You look just like I left you!"

"Thanks a lot Sydney. I'm short and chunky, you mean?"

"You're always beautiful, Becky, and you know it!"

"Okay, okay, I'll stop while *I'm* ahead," Becky joked. "Bet you haven't eaten a thing all day, have you?"

"I, ah, I guess I haven't, now that you mention it."

"Good, cause I'm starving, let's have a sandwich and visit for a bit, before we get too involved in packing." Becky made herself at home as she started busying herself with the sandwich making, while Sydney poured them both a glass of iced tea and set the table.

Neither one of them spoke much as they enjoyed their sandwiches. Sydney didn't know if Becky was aware of her marital problems or not, still keeping the fact that Margie had stopped over to herself. She didn't really think so, because Becky wasn't the kind to keep that kind of information from her. Then again, Jeff wasn't the type to call his mother and fill her in on all of their dirty laundry either, but he did.

"How's the shop doing?" Sydney inquired. Her father had left her his half of the shop after he and Randy had become partners, but she had no interest in it. So Randy had been making payments to her religiously, to pay it off, and he was getting pretty close.

"Oh, I almost forgot!" Becky exclaimed as she unzipped her purse and pulled out an envelope. "He wanted me to give this to you today. He's very proud of himself I might add!" as she handed Sydney the envelope.

Sydney carefully opened the envelope and after looking at the amount written on the check, raised her eyebrows in surprise. "Wow, guess that answers my question!"

"Yep! I'm so proud of him; he's been working so hard. This, I know, is a relief for him. Speaking of husbands, how's Jeff doing? It's really too bad that he wasn't able to break away and come with you. It would have been nice for us all to get together."

Becky always had a habit of talking so quickly that from the time words left her lips to Sydney's ears was like watching lightening strike and waiting for the roar of thunder. Sydney replied that Jeff was doing fine and that he had told her to tell everyone hello for him. Which was a slight fib, he wasn't doing fine, nor was she, but he did ask her to tell everyone hello for him. Sydney didn't say anymore, just quickly changed the subject.

"Okay, where do you want me?" Becky said as she clapped her hands once.

"I've been concentrating on the upstairs for right now. I thought it might be best to get that all moved and cleaned out, before dealing with the downstairs. I haven't brought any of the boxes that I've already packed downstairs yet, but they are ready. So if you want, we can move those into the garage, so they're not in our way?"

"Sounds like a good plan! We probably won't get much farther than that today, anyhow. No sense in wearing ourselves out the first day!" giggled Becky.

To both their surprise, they did get a lot farther than either one of them anticipated. Sydney was thankful for all of this work to keep her mind and hands busy. It lifted some of the depression that she had been feeling. After they were finished,

Becky told Sydney that she would be back the next morning, while adding that she had better had breakfast ready. Sydney gave Becky a mock salute and clicked her heels, as Becky was stepping back out into the rain. With a wave and a run, she was gone.

CHAPTER *twenty-three*

The house seemed impossibly quiet after Becky left. Sydney was tired from her day, as she walked slowly back upstairs to go to bed. She didn't have enough energy left to even take a shower, so instead, just changed back into her pajamas. Sydney reached for her duffel bag that she had brought with her and pulled out the old picture of her mother. She stared at her smiling face, knowing that picture was taken just shortly before she died and wondering what she could have possibly been so happy about. Sydney slowly turned it over and read the words *Always in your heart, Love, Mom.* How she wished she had her to talk to right now.

With the rain still steadily hitting the window pane of her bedroom, she climbed into the softness of her bed. She lay there, listening to the rain, looking into the darkness and replaying Margie's words to her. Sydney began talking into the darkness. *God, if you're really here, with me, knowing how I'm feeling right now, then please help me. I need your help. I don't want to feel like this anymore. Please, please.* Sydney wiped her tears away and drifted off into a far away place.

The next morning, Sydney was awakened to the sunlight shooting through her window. She slowly opened her eyes, squinting from the light and smiled. Sydney felt a lightness inside her heart that she hadn't felt in a very long time as she stepped out of bed. Remembering Becky's request for breakfast, that's exactly what Sydney was going to do for her helping her. She jumped into the shower quickly, feeling refreshed and clean. She placed the sausage that she had cooked into the oven on low, to keep it warm until Becky arrived.

Becky knocked shortly after Sydney had brought the eggs out of the refrigerator and placed four pieces of bread out next to the toaster. Sydney let her in as Becky strode through the living room smelling the sausage.

"Boy that smell is like heaven to my hips! I don't know about you, but I'm starving! If you only knew how hard I worked to maintain these hips I've acquired, you'd be amazed," Becky joked.

She and Becky worked hard the next two days, working from early in the morning till late into the night. They sorted through everything that wasn't nailed down, throwing out some things, while placing what was left into the pile marked personal, which were the things that Sydney wanted to keep, and the other pile that was to be donated. Neither one of them moved any of the furniture, leaving that for the movers. Even with the furniture in tact, the house looked stripped. Becky noted the sadness that swept over Sydney's face.

"How 'bout you come and stay the night with me and Randy?"

"No, I'd like to stay here. I know it sounds kind of silly, but I kind of feel like I'm leaving a very good friend, forever."

"I understand, Syd. I'll be back again tomorrow, to help you tie up any loose ends. Of course, it won't be quite as early, I'm pooped!" Becky smiled as she stretched her back while rubbing her shoulder.

"Yeah, me too," Sydney said softly.

"Okay, unless you need anything else, I'm going to take off now?"

"Nope, not unless you wanna stay and give my back a much needed massage?"

"I'm outta here!" Becky laughed on her way out.

"Thanks Becky, I'll see ya tomorrow."

CHAPTER *twenty-four*

For the next couple of days, Jeff would only pop into the office when he had an appointment and to pick up more work to take with him home. Finally, after a few days of doing this, he stepped into the office to talk with his partner. He told him that he needed a few days off due to a family emergency. His partner was a kind man that knew Jeff had been through a lot in these last few months and without hesitating told him to take all the time he needed. Jeff went over the particulars of the cases that he had been working on, what needed attention first and so on.

Jeff briefed his secretary that he would be gone for a few days, informing her that if something urgent came up, to contact Dave. Jeff could hardly wait to get out of the office, before taking a deep breath of the crisp cool Colorado air outside. Once home, he set his plan in motion.

Sydney let her mind float back in time as she strolled around the house. The memories making her emotions rise and fall. As tired as she was, Sydney stayed up late into the night, doing a lot of thinking and praying. She even thought about calling Jeff, but changed her mind. She wasn't ready, as much as she wanted to be ready. A great fear of Jeff saying the words out loud that she knew they were both thinking, was simply terrifying for her. *Sure Jeff called his mother, saying how worried he was about me, but that's how Jeff is to everyone. That doesn't mean he wants to fix our marriage. He probably just wanted to ease his conscious. He probably wants to wait to file for divorce as soon as he knows I won't fly off the deep end. Or wait the necessary amount of time, so that he won't look like the bad guy, filing for divorce only a few months after my baby died.* Sydney felt the anger start to rise like an awful bile. She slipped into her bed, wanting the world to disappear, as these thoughts consumed her mind. *Please help me, God. I need your help.* Sydney started repeating this phrase as if she were saying a mantra, until finally, the sleep that she longed for, took hold of her.

Jeff's plane landed in Chicago, at the O'Hare airport at 4:33 a.m. He rented a car to drive the rest of the way. It was another three to four hours before he'd be there and he was exhausted, but shrugged off stopping at a hotel. Jeff figured that if he got too tired, then he'd just pull over at a rest area and take a nap. The lack of sleep and the emotional upheaval that he'd been through had started to take its toll. He began questioning his decision to come here, but if nothing else came of it, he still could visit Jacob's grave.

As he pulled into their small town that morning, he embraced the memories. Jeff didn't even stop at his mother's house, he drove directly to Sydney's father's house. He barely noticed the leaves covering the lawns, or the chill in the air. His rental car rounded the corner and from there he could see a vehicle in the driveway. It was still early in the morning, but light was dusting the earth. Jeff slowed the car to a crawl as he pulled into the driveway. Having a sudden case of nerves, he walked up to the front door, finding it locked, rang the doorbell.

Sydney was still dozing comfortably when she heard the

doorbell. With a slight irritation, Sydney pushed the covers away and went to answer the door. As she opened the door with the same irritation she was feeling and looked up, finding her husband standing there. Her mouth dropped open.

"J . . . Jeff, wh . . . what are you doing here?" Sydney felt as if someone had a vice grip on her stomach.

"We need to talk, Syd," was all Jeff could manage.

Sydney backed away from the doorway to allow Jeff entry. He stopped as he looked around the house. Then he looked into her eyes as she looked back into his, seeing the first time his pain. She noticed the dark circles under Jeff's eyes, looking as if he hadn't slept for a week. His hair looked as if he had been running his fingers through it constantly and the creases around his eyes were more distinct.

Suddenly self-conscious, Sydney excused herself to run up the stairs and grab her robe. Sydney quickly gave herself the once over in the bathroom mirror, immediately wishing she hadn't. She looked horrible, her face was pale, her eyes were swollen, and her hair looked as if it hadn't been combed in days. When Sydney made her way back down to the bottom of the stairs, she found Jeff in the kitchen pouring water into the coffee pot.

The brewing of the coffee was making its gurgling sounds as Sydney sat at the table. Neither one of them spoke, pretending that they couldn't see the stain that had spread through the fabric of their lives. Sydney still sat there in shocked silence, staring down at the floor, with Jeff sitting across from her. Jeff suddenly got up, opening all the drawers in the kitchen and finding them all empty, while searching for a spoon.

Reading his mind, Sydney spoke. "To your far right there's some plastic silverware. Becky and I have already packed away everything else."

"Thanks." He glanced her way out of the corner of his eye,

as he grabbed one and poured the coffee into a styrofoam cup. "Here, it looks like you could use a little."

"That bad, huh?" Sydney, suddenly defeated, replied sarcastically.

Jeff didn't take the bait, merely continued to pour himself some coffee. He walked to the table, stirring the cream, watching it swirl around in circles. He didn't seat himself on the other side of the table this time either, he sat right next to Sydney.

Sydney was uncomfortable with the closeness and scooted her chair away from him. Jeff turned his chair sideways, facing her when he leaned back in his chair and stared at her. He crossed his legs, picked up his coffee, taking a sip, and continued to stare.

"Jeff, just say what you need to say and then I'd appreciate it if you'd let yourself out," Sydney said, surprised at her own anger and uncomfortable with his eyes on her.

"Look at me, Sydney; do you honestly think that I'm going anywhere? I didn't come all this way to say a few things to you, then walk out and go home, as if I lived down on the next block! I'm not going any place soon, until we open up some form of communication, without sarcasm and hatefulness. We've done that and that didn't work, so let's try a new approach. I'll start.

"I love you. I love you more than you could ever know or will allow yourself to know. I know that I've been distant, even to the point of seeming cold. Since Jacob's death, we've both been wandering around lost. I miss him horribly, as I know you do. We've handled our sadness differently, me by working so much, and you by closing yourself off to everyone and trying to get through it on your own. You know a couple of days ago, I remembered something that Gretta had told me years and years ago, when my dad first left. She told me that when people were hurt, it was much like having a skinned knee. She said that when people were hurt on the inside, they did the same thing we do when we skin our knee. They cover it up with a bandage, so that the injury will be protected from anything else making it hurt more. Sometimes people forget to take the bandage off, for fear of increasing their pain. So they keep wearing it, thinking that they are protecting themselves.

"In order for it to heal, though, it needs to have air, needs to breathe. She told me that when it hits the air, the healing will start, but even while it's healing, it sometimes can hurt more than it did before. It becomes tight and red around the injury, making it tender to the touch. But then it gets smaller and smaller until it's nothing but fresh new skin, helping it to become a distant memory. Sydney, what we need to do is to take the bandage off now. I know the pain is not going to go away today, tomorrow, or the next day, but it will *never* lessen if we don't let it heal. Pain has a lot of side effects that come along with it, like, despair, anger, self destructive behaviors, fear, anxiety, loneliness, and the list goes on and on. So by removing pain, you are also removing all of the side-effects. I've let not only our relationship go, but I've let my own relationship with God go, too. I am prepared to leave, if that's what you want in your heart, but I'm even more prepared to stay and give you an endless supply of love. I suppose I'll give it to you either way, just didn't want the leaving part to look too good to you," Jeff said with an attempt at humor.

Sydney smiled and for the first time in many months, reached her hand out and took her husband's hand, feeling all the anger seep away as if it were rain on a dry desert floor. "Jeff, I loved you yesterday, I love you today, and I will love you tomorrow and all the days to follow. You are right, I need to take the bandage off and let myself heal properly. The thing is, it's going to take some time. I'm not capable of making the decisions you're asking me to make right now. I can't tell you right this very moment that I'm coming back, because I'm not ready to. I don't expect you to wait for the day when I'm ready, nor do I want you to. It's just too fresh right now. Sometimes I'm afraid that when I let go of all my sadness that I'm in some way letting go of Jacob, too. Right now, I want to keep him with me."

Jeff felt as if a door had been slammed shut in his face. He was so confident that he could make things right. He had wanted this so badly, that the very thought of having to leave back to Colorado alone, was unbearable to him. Jeff fought off the sudden urge to yell at her, to shake some sense into her, when the realization hit him. He had been praying, asking God to give him peace in his life. When in reality, he had been asking God for what *he* specifically wanted, not for what God wanted from him. Now Jeff found himself perplexed, sitting here in this somewhat surreal situation. *God, you've lost me now buddy. What am I supposed to do now?* Jeff thought to himself.

Jeff spoke, "I understand, Sydney. You take all the time you need, I won't push you anymore. I don't ever want you coming back because you were pushed into it, instead I'd rather wait until you *want* to come back. I still meant everything that I told you and am not reneging on how I would love you no matter what. Although if I thought for a moment that placing a condition on my love for you would actually work, can't say that I might not give it a shot." Smiling, Jeff continued. "Sydney, whatever you decide to do is your decision, but I want to say one more thing to you before I leave."

Jeff rested his elbows on his knees as he dropped his head for a moment, then lifted his eyes to Sydney's. "I'm going to be brutally honest with you; I'm not happy with your response. I suppose I thought that we'd just fall into each other's arms and set out walking into the sunset together, happily ever after.

Before we were married, I had made a very important promise to God. I told Him that I loved and appreciated Him so very much, that no matter what, He would always be number one in my life. Well, I lied. I put everything else in front of Him and in doing so, lost my closeness with Him that had pulled me through so many difficulties in my life. Back then, I had faith in His infinite wisdom. Somewhere down the line, I slowly started dismissing Him. My pride and arrogance started kicking back in and I began making my own decisions without talking with Him about them. I wanted to handle things on my own. The joy that used to light my heart like a campfire has burned out, leaving nothing but the residue. It's as if I were having all of these parties and never inviting my best friend to any of them. I very likely may end up losing you and I will deal with that if or when that happens, but I'll never lose my God again, because that I could not deal with. If you promise me nothing else, please keep God close to you, don't allow anything or anyone to come between that friendship with Him."

Jeff stood. "Well, I suppose that I best be going."

"Where are you going to go?"

"To sleep," Jeff snickered, as he grabbed his coat. "I'll be at my mom's for a few days, might as well take advantage of some of this time off to visit with her. She has no idea that I'm here, so I imagine she'll be pretty surprised at seeing me at her door."

"You didn't tell anyone you were coming here?" Sydney looked surprised.

"Nope, well, with the exception of my partner, of course. I don't think that I even knew myself, until I got here!" Leaning over to Sydney, he kissed her cheek, touched her face softly and left.

CHAPTER *twenty-five*

Jeff didn't go straight to his mother's house. He drove in the direction of the graveyard, where Sydney's parents and his baby boy, Jacob, were buried, by their sides. Nearing the turn that led to the graveyard, his heart began pulsating with a great deep sadness. He literally felt as if he had to drag his feet to the gravesite. He pulled up his jacket collar from the chill in the breeze, while shoving his hands in his pockets. He touched Sally's grave, then Charles, as if saying hello. He then squatted to little Jacobs. *Hey pal, it's me pop's. Bet you're having a ball with grandpa and grandma or sitting on God's lap, with his arms wrapped around you. You're a pretty lucky little guy, to have so much love.* Jeff coughed a couple of times, to clear his throat, then he bowed his head and began to pray. *Lord, I'm so lost right now. I know that you've got plans for me. I know that with you, I will get through this. I miss Jacob so much; please take good care of him for me. Now I'm handing my life back over to you, please accept it. Your will is my will. I trust my life to you. Fill my heart with your love again, I need you now. Right now!* Jeff was still squatted down, with so many tears pouring down his face, that he couldn't speak anymore.

It was in that deepest and darkest moment of despair that

Jeff felt such an emotion roll up throughout his body, from the very tips of his toes, to the scalp of his head, that it brought more tears to his eyes. Never had he ever felt such a powerful feeling in his life hit him with the force that this one had. It wasn't just a peace that filled his heart, but a love that filled his heart as a blinding burst of sunshine. *I must be losing my mind,* Jeff thought to himself as he laughed with joy.

Nothing could surpass this incredible feeling of love. Jeff no longer had the hunger in his heart, it had been sated. With tears streaming down his face, he thought he surely must have finally crossed the line from sanity to insanity. The joy was inexplicable; the warmth of love he felt inside was overwhelming. In that one moment, Jeff knew that his life had changed forever. He wasn't going to lose this absurd feeling. God had answered him, instantly, just as he had asked Him to. Even the fact that no one experienced it with him didn't matter. He finally knew, after all of those years of *thinking* he knew, that he really hadn't. This was the first time in his life, that he handed his life, completely and totally, into God's hands. Sure he used to let him have part of it, granted it was usually the problem part, but never had Jeff given everything, not like this. Jeff's wife didn't appear, his life didn't become perfect, his son was still dead, but yet this undeniable feeling of love filled his heart, till he thought it would surely burst. Somehow, Jeff knew that he had made the right choice and that he would be fine no matter what happened in his life.

Jeff left the graveyard no longer shackled with the constraints of negative emotions that he left Colorado with. Even as tired and weary as he was he noticed all the loveliness of the world. He walked up the short walkway to his mother's little house, feeling invincible, powerful, and the most wonderful feeling of all, was that he finally felt deeply and truly loved.

Rather than turn the knob to see if her door was unlocked,

he rang the bell. As his mother opened the door, she gasped while flinging her hand to her chest. Jeff leaned down to her and they hugged. "It's good to be home, Mom."

Margie looked into Jeff's eyes, looking for remnants of what he was feeling and found none. Jeff told her of his decision to come visit, leaving out what had transpired between Sydney and him, just simply saying that they both needed a little time to work through the puzzle of their lives.

Margie realized that Jeff must be exhausted and pushed him into his old bedroom. His room was the same as he left it, with poster's hanging on the wall as any other normal teenager had. His graduation tassle still hung over the corner of the mirror on his dresser. A couple of trophies that he had gotten for baseball, still sat on an old second hand book case that his mother had found for him at a garage sale. An old baseball cap was still slung over his headboard. His baseball bat and mitt still sat in the corner, by his closet.

Margie pulled the covers back for him and gave him another hug and kiss, as she quietly told him she'd wake him in a few hours, after she had dinner made. She quietly blew him another kiss from the doorway, as she closed it softly behind her. As Jeff grabbed something to change into out of his suitcase, he realized that he never remembered his mother doing this for him as a child. *How crazy our lives can be,* Jeff thought to himself as he changed. Jeff fell asleep before his head ever hit the pillow.

After Jeff left, Sydney wandered listless around the old house. Sydney thought about how Jeff just threw all of his feelings out into the wind. Never had Jeff been so open, never letting himself be so vulnerable. Sydney thought about all that he had said to her. More importantly, she couldn't let go of what he said at the end, about not letting anything come between her and God. *I never did let anything come between us. God did.*

He didn't care enough to keep my mother alive, my dad alive, and even took my baby. Sydney knew this was one of the reasons why she couldn't go home with Jeff, because to be honest, she was fed up.

Hey God, if you're listening, then listen closely! You haven't been my best friend, ever. You've never given me anything, only took and took and took, until I have nothing left for you to take from me! So yeah, now you've taken my husband, too! Well, I guess all you have left to take is me, how do you like that? Sydney was trembling with rage. For the last few days she had gone back and forth emotionally so many times, that she was never sure what she'd be feeling the next moment. She wanted to throw something, anything, but everything had been packed up. The despair came back, feeling as if it were slicing her in two. Sydney had had enough; enough hiding, enough adjusting the mask of happiness, enough performing, enough of everything. She had never been so thoroughly exhausted in her entire life.

Sydney was vicariously teetering on the edge of the will to live versus the will to die. The burden of anger had become far too heavy for her to bear on her own. She couldn't walk another step of life. This was something that she could control, she had the wheel of her own life and no one was going to take it from her. Sydney made her way upstairs to find the tranquilizer's that the doctor had prescribed to her when Jacob died. Not knowing why she had brought them with, she searched with her hand until she pulled them out and stared at them long and hard. Making a conscious decision, Sydney slowly removed the cap.

CHAPTER *twenty-six*

Jeff was stirring out of his deep sleep with an aroma coming from the kitchen of his mother's home. As he rolled over onto his back, he stared at the ceiling, thinking how much his mother had changed. She made him proud of her. After working so diligently with other women that were fighting for their very existence, he understood their fears, anxieties, and low self-confidence. Seeing his mother succeed like this was exhilarating for him. She had overcome so much. She was a success story in herself. No, she didn't have riches, fame, or notoriety, but she had something far more valuable, she had herself, her confidence, her peace of mind, and her faith. To him she would always be a hero. Success, he supposed, was measured from the eyes that were viewing it. To some, success was measured in monetary value, careers, and how big their houses, cars, and toys were. To him, success was what he felt in his heart earlier that day. Success was having the love he had been given.

The mouthwatering smell drove Jeff out of his comfort. While standing in the shower letting the hot water pelt into his back, he felt renewed. Walking into the small kitchen, Jeff glanced around the little house that he and his mother had shared so long ago, after leaving the other one. Even though it was tiny, it contained a warmth. She had done a lot to it since he had seen it the last time, as he noticed the little knick-knacks appearing in tiny corners that were once empty.

"Did you get plenty of sleep, Hon?"

"I don't know if it was plenty, but it felt good. I probably wouldn't have woken up for four more days if I didn't smell something delicious brewing in here," Jeff responded as he lifted the lid of the pot to glimpse the contents while his mother was cutting tomato's for a nice big green salad that she had prepared.

"Git, Git, Git!" His mother lightly paddled his hand with her wooden spoon, jokingly.

"Spaghetti, eh? When did you learn how to make spaghetti?"

"When Gretta came over one evening for dinner and didn't like what I cooked. Actually, I believe that it was one of the first times I've ever laughed so hard. She took one bite of the food that I made and looked as if she were going to become viciously ill. After she had regained her composure, she told me that at least I got even with your father by cooking for him," Margie said, laughing at the memory. "You know, that Gretta, she's a real character. She's one of those people that hands out her opinions like brightly wrapped gifts topped with a beautiful bow, waiting for the person receiving it to open it and be joyful, as if it's something they have always wanted."

Jeff started laughing with his mother. "Yeah, that sounds exactly like Gretta. How's she doing these days anyhow? Has anyone been to visit her lately?"

"I was just there yesterday afternoon. I stop by there as often as I can. Her sons are wonderful boys. Every single time I've popped in there, one of them is always there by her bed-side. But, I don't think that she's doing so well lately. It's funny though, yesterday while I was there, she kept telling me that she would be seeing John soon? Who's John, Jeff, do you know?"

Jeff felt chills run along his spine. "That's her husband that died years ago."

"Oh my, I can't believe it, because she seemed to be so lucid when she told me that."

"Maybe she was."

"Oh honey, you certainly don't think . . ." Margie left her thoughts hang in the air.

"Gretta's a very smart and strong woman. I wouldn't be surprised one bit if she knew something that we didn't. After all, she's always seemed to have a *box seat* where God is concerned."

"Gretta's always, well, she's just always been such a boost to have around. I don't think that I could have made it those first few weeks without her support. Everyone just loves her so."

"What gets you through now, Mom?" he asked as he leaned his back against the counter, itching to tell her of his experience.

Margie turned to him, "Why I thought that you knew?"

"I think that I do, but why don't you tell me anyhow." Jeff watched her place the noodles into the boiling water and stick the garlic bread into the oven.

After she finished with her tasks, her cheeks were flushed from the warmth of the oven as she stood up. "Why don't you sit down and I'll tell you everything that you want to know." Margie placed the oven mitts on the kitchen table in front of her while she sat down too. Margie began to tell Jeff her story, at times having to pause from the memories.

CHAPTER *twenty-seven*

After opening the bottle of tranquilizers, Sydney poured them all into her palm. Her anger wasn't just simmering underneath her surface anymore; it had come to a full raging boil, where it could no longer be hidden anymore. Staring down into the palm of her hand, she was able to embody what those who had tried to take their own lives and wheeled into the emergency room were undergoing. They would beg her to let them slip into the only peace that they thought they could find, sometimes grabbing her shirt, sometimes hitting her hands away, anything that they were able to do to allow themselves to escape the misery that they felt would never go away. Sydney always wondered what could be so awful in their minds that they would go to this length to escape it. She now knew it was anger and emptiness. An anger that was so intense, that not only were they punishing themselves, but everyone around them. They were lashing out. It was an emptiness so very deep, that it seemed endless.

They had never taken their bandage off, Sydney thought. *They had internalized their pain. They weren't just keeping it close; they were embracing it so tightly that no one, nothing could come between them, just like me. I'm always pretending I don't have it and when someone suspects that I do, I try to push it down even far-ther, away from their eyes. It's become like a jack in the box, you can only push it down for so long, with time being the one turning the arm of that jack in the box, and it pops back out, it will always pop back out.* Sydney slowly walked to the bathroom and turned her palm upside down over the toilet, watching the pills float to the bottom. Looking at them settle on the bottom, she pushed the knob and flushed them all away. Sydney then walked to the phone and called Becky.

"Hello?" Becky answered on the first ring, as if she had been sitting right next to the phone.

"Hi Becky, this is Sydney. Are you busy right now?"

"Not at all, in fact, I was just getting ready to call you, Syd. I was going to literally force you out of that house to come on over here for dinner tonight. I haven't heard from you all day? What have you been doing?"

"That's kind of why I called. I want to talk to you about that."

"Do you want me to come pick you up, or do you want to drive?"

"Oh, I can just drive over there."

"Well, bring some overnight clothes, cause there's no rea-son for you to go back to that big 'ole house by yourself."

"Okay, I'll bring some, but if I change my mind, don't get mad?"

"Syd, have I *ever* been mad at you?"

"I don't think you've ever been mad in your life, Becky. Listen, I'll be over in about a half an hour, is that all right?"

"Super!"

Hanging the phone up, Sydney felt as if she were remov-ing the first stone of this mountain that stood in front of her. She had finally loosened the corner of her bandage. She took a quick shower, made herself presentable, grabbing the few things that she would need and made her way to Becky's house.

Upon arriving, Becky as exuberant as ever, greeted her as she did the first day of Sydney's arrival. They settled Sydney's things into the guest bedroom, while Becky explained that Randy would probably be at the shop for another couple of hours.

Settling in the living room, Becky sensed something going on with Sydney and remained silent. Sydney was hesitant at first, while releasing the emotions that had been imprisoned and carried for so long, that just saying them, literally made Sydney feel lighter. Becky remained silent while Sydney opened her heart to her and bared it, sometimes with embarrassment, other times defensive, but most of the time with vulnerability, tears, and desperation. Becky's heart went out to Sydney, as she went to her and hugged her.

Sydney had spilled all the ugliness she had kept inside for so long out. Becky took a moment, before she spoke to this woman who sat before her as broken as the abused women that she had counseled for so long. Becky realized that the pain and despair that people felt in their hearts came from so many directions, not just one.

"Sydney, you have every right to feel this way. It's kind of like wearing shoes that don't fit. They're too small, too big, too something, but we continue walking in them anyhow, because they're the only one's we have. Why don't we go out and buy another pair? Well, because sometimes we become emotionally *bankrupt*, we can't afford another pair. That's where I'm going to have to agree with Jeff. If you reach out for God, you will find He's right next to you, handing you a brand new pair of shoes that won't cause you the discomfort that the one's you're wearing do. He'll even put them on for you, but He won't do it unless you let Him. It's not because He's unkind or doesn't want us to walk through this life comfortably, but because He has given us the freedom of choice."

"Sydney, God is crazy in love with you. As many times as you turn your back on Him, He will take you back, each and every time. He will not say to you, "*Now where have you been? I want you to answer for yourself, young lady!*" He is so excessively in love with you that nothing matters to Him, except the fact that He has you back in His arms. He doesn't stop there; no He doesn't just take you back into His arms, but He lavishes you with gifts that only He can afford. He has an endless amount of wealth, an infinite amount, it never ends. He's telling you to grab as much as you want, take it freely."

"Right now Syd, you're in the trenches fighting with all of these demons who are better armed than you are; you will not win on your own. By allowing God into your life, He will whip every one of those demons with one arm tied behind His back. He will not only do that, but He will make sure that they don't come back, no matter what bridge you have to cross in your lifetime. He will keep you safe. You will have trials throughout your life, but with Him you will walk right through them with the ease and finesse of a model walking down the runway."

Sydney wiped her nose and tears with the sleeve of the sweatshirt that she was wearing. Quietly, Sydney whispered, "I want Him back. Will you help me?"

"Sugar, the moment you spoke those words, He was back. God is a rather overzealous fellow, you know. Can't you feel Him moving into your heart, Sydney? Right now He's probably discarding some of that old ugly furniture in there and making way for His own beautiful things and making a lot of noise while doing it."

Sydney's eyes were shining with tears. She leaned over and hugged Becky as a booming voice behind them, made them jump.

"What's going on here?" Randy's lanky body strolled into the room smiling, as Sydney stood up to hug him.

"How's my favorite little gal?" He planted a kiss on her cheek. Stepping back with concern, he wiped a stray tear from Sydney's cheek, looking towards Becky questioningly.

"We were just reminiscing about some old friends," Becky interjected, seeing the gratefulness in Sydney's face for not having to explain.

"How's Jeff doing, Syd?"

Becky interjected again, saving the day yet again. "Sydney told me that Jeff surprised her by coming to town this morning. He's at his mother's visiting with her tonight."

"Really, well I would like to see him while he's here! How longs he gonna be here, Sydney? Maybe if he's going to be here a while, he could come and work for me a couple of days. After all, I'd like to see him get those *baby soft attorney's hands* dirty again," Randy smugly said, while giving Sydney a wink.

"Gee, Randy, you seem to be doing quite well on your own, by the check Becky gave to me. Besides, I'm really not quite sure as to how long he'll be staying; he told me a few days, but that may change."

"Well, then, I'm thinking that maybe a cookout is in order tomorrow night. We'll have to invite Margie, too, of course."

"It's freezing outside, Randy! I hope you're planning on doing the grilling! Besides, I think you should really make sure that it's okay with them first, before making all of these plans."

"Of course I will!" Randy looked to Sydney, while rolling his eyes to the ceiling.

That night after going to bed, Sydney curled herself up tightly in the blankets. *I see now the blessings that I've been overlooking all along.*

CHAPTER *twenty-eight*

Jeff talked with his mother after filling himself up with spaghetti. He helped her do the dishes, as she washed and he dried. He listened to her chatter. They went into the living room and continued talking late into the night, until his eyes grazed over the clock on the wall, realizing the late hour, and they said their goodnight's to each other.

The next morning, Jeff found his mother on the phone. She pointed at a cereal box on the counter. "Well, let me check with Jeff and I'll get back to you as soon as I find out." With a few more words, she hung the phone up smiling.

"Who was that?" Jeff asked, as he was sure that no one besides Sydney knew he was here, his heart doing a flip flop of hope.

"Honey, that was Becky wanting you and I over for dinner tonight." Margie smiled with gleam. "It seems that your wife stayed over at their house last night and told them that you were here. That's good news isn't it?"

"Or maybe, she just told them that I was here because she figured that they'd find out anyhow."

Margie frowned. "Oh, don't be so pessimistic!"

"I'm not, mom, but I just don't think that it's a good idea to get my hopes up again. After all, you make me spaghetti from scratch last night that I might add was out of this world. Then you want to feed me cereal the next morning, if that isn't a balloon bursting, then I don't know what is!" Jeff joked dryly. "So let me take you out for breakfast this morning, mom."

"You've got yourself a deal."

Sydney left Becky's house that morning to wait for the movers. Becky said that she'd be over in about an hour to help. Sydney didn't know what she was going to do with the furniture quite yet, so she had arranged for it to be moved to a storage unit, until she could decide. She took all the bedding off of her bed that she had left on there to sleep in. Becky had helped her to dismantle her parent's bed, leaning the mattresses up against the wall, taking apart the headboard and such. Sydney was struggling with the top mattress, trying to manipulate it into going the way she wanted it to, when she saw Jeff standing in her doorway watching her, scaring her half to death.

"Don't just stand there, get over here and help me with this stupid thing, will ya," Sydney snapped.

"Sounds like home," Jeff retorted, smiling.

Sydney stopped, almost getting toppled over by the mattress as Jeff reached for it just before it collapsed on top of her. "Are you going to help me or not, Jeff?"

"Sydney, I've been wanting to help you for years, just was waiting for you to finally let me. Yes, I'll help you, if you promise to ask a little nicer next time."

They both left words unspoken hover between them, as Sydney said in a soft voice, "I promise."

CHAPTER *twenty-nine*

Jeff and Sydney still had many stones to move before they would begin to see results. Each had their own separate relationship with Jesus that they shared with one another. After that morning, they both had walked from the darkness into the light, with their hands clasped tightly. They had many bumps, hills, and mountains stand before them that no longer stopped them from getting to the other side.

The difference in Jeff was as Sydney remembered seeing in her father. It was the same subtle change that she noticed in him. It was in the same smiling face of her mother in that picture that she carried with her for so many years. It was even in Jacob's smile and eyes right before he ran into the road. How could she have missed something so thoroughly blatant? It was a great, powerful love that put the sparkle in their eyes, the laughter in their hearts, and the joy in their faces. It couldn't be explained, no matter how she tried.

She and Jeff had walked into another journey of their lives. They walked through, leaving behind all the doubts, fears, and anger that had become an anchor that had not only slowed them down to a standstill, but would have certainly drowned them both, had they not clasped their hands into God's out-stretched one.

When Sydney found she was pregnant again, she felt terror in the beginning. Before she would allow herself to ask for reassurance from God, she felt His love surround her as a fortress, washing that fear away. Sydney felt a great peace in her heart. She had no doubt that He would catch her if she started falling, she believed in Him, trusted in Him, and loved Him. *That note that Margie read to her was right, He really will take us places we never believed possible to go.*

Sydney watched Jeff's attention turn towards cooking steaks out on the grill, while she sat in the warmth of the Colorado sunlight, letting it bathe her. Her stomach had grown, to where her pregnancy was noticed by others. Although she wished that she still had little Jacob, he would always be locked away inside of her heart. She no longer carried the guilt and anger around as she used to. Now she was filled with the knowledge, that some day, she would see him again.

Sydney smiled, while she thought about her life. *Each and every event of my life happened for a reason. How would I have ever arrived at this destination, had I not gone through all of the other's to get here? God has attended to each and every detail of my life, to the point of being obsessively compulsive. His timing is impeccable.* Jeff boyishly grinned as he walked towards Sydney carrying the plate holding the two steaks.

"So what're you gonna eat?" Sydney joked.

"That's funny, because I was going to ask you the very same question," as he stooped down to kiss his pregnant wife, while patting her belly.

The phone rang, interrupting their laughter. Jeff stepped through the sliding glass doors to answer the phone. "Hello?" His eyes turned to Sydney and then he lowered his voice and turned away from Sydney.

Sydney felt her finger's clutch the arms of the chair she was seated in, as she waited.

Jeff stepped back out of the sliding glass doors and sat down in the chair by Sydney, taking both of her hands into his. Looking directly into her eyes, his lips began moving as Sydney watched them, waiting for the sound from them to hit her ears.

"Sydney, that was my mom. God has taken Gretta home."

Sydney reached for Jeff. He held her in his arms as she cried many tears, some of sadness at losing her beloved friend, some from the joy that she had at knowing she finally would be reunited with her husband, but more importantly from the fact that she was finally home, in God's arms. After each of them let go of each other, not being able to shed one more tear, they held hands while they said a prayer for Gretta and for her sons.

Jeff and Sydney flew back home for her funeral. Sydney had no idea how many lives Gretta had touched through the years, but was amazed at the attendance. The unmarried son's speech was the most touching that Sydney had ever heard.

He approached the podium, his face alive with all of the raw emotion that he was feeling. As he looked out into the sea of faces, he began:

> "I'm going to start out by telling all of you that my mother has run a close second to God, in my life. I am sad, because I will miss her for these remaining years that I've left on this earth, but I am not sad for her. She is home now. She has always been here, to be the wall, when I needed one to lean on. She has been the speed bump, when she needed to slow me down. She's been my hurdle, when she wanted to see how high I

could jump. She's been my cheerleader, when I needed a fan. She's been my shoulder, when I needed one to cry on. She's been my nurse, when I've been hurt and the list goes on and on.

"As I look out here, at so many faces, some familiar, some not, I finally see what my mother has left behind. I don't know the role that she has played in many of your lives, but I do know that having her in your life at all, is a great blessing in and of itself. I will see my mother again, like she always said, 'Good things come to those who wait.' She spent her whole life waiting for this moment and I imagine heaven is being turned upside down with her appearance." Sydney joined everyone in giggles, as she looked to Jeff.

"My mom was many things to me, but fearful was not one of them. She spent every moment of her life reaching out to others, letting them in on her secret 'happiness recipe.' God made no mistake when he chose my mother for his team, nor did she, in accepting His offer. One thing she always told me was that when you were on God's team, there wasn't a chance that you'd lose and she's right. She told me once that the one request my father had asked of her was that she make a difference in just one person's life." He paused for a moment, before continuing.

"So, as I stand here now, looking at all of these faces in front of me, I believe that she did indeed make that difference. I am so proud of her. What she has left behind is a message for us. That message is telling us that we, too, have the power to touch other's lives in a positive way.

My mother always called it the 'ripple effect,' for everything we do throughout our lives will affect someone else's.

"God, I think that you've got your hands full. Take care of mom and dad for us. Well mom, I hope that I've done you proud, I love you."

The most moving thing Sydney had ever felt happened in that church that summer day. As Gretta's son started to leave the podium, Gretta's other two sons stood up and started clapping, with tears streaming down their faces. Others followed suit and started standing and clapping. Gretta was receiving a standing ovation. A woman had slipped to the corner microphone and started singing "Amazing Grace" acapella with a strong beautiful voice. Sydney felt a spirit move through her heart, like nothing she had ever experienced before. Looking around, she could tell that others felt it, too. Jeff looked down at Sydney. She was crying like a child and placed his arm around her, hugging her close to his side.

"You feel his love, don't you?" he whispered knowingly.

Sydney could only nod, not trusting her voice to speak. This was such a strange feeling, but not one she wanted to leave anytime soon. She finally understood.

Jeff and Sydney flew back a day after the funeral, giving them both time to enjoy with their friends and family. They had all gone over to Becky and Randy's home, which seemed now to be the new meeting place. The weather was clear and warm, with summer's polite entry. Jeff stood over the grill with Randy, while flipping burgers. Jeff glanced over to his pregnant wife sitting out in the lawn chair with his mother and Becky, laughing and looking relaxed. As she caught his eyes, he noticed the *twinkle* in her topaz one's, while she mouthed the words, *I love you*, to him. Margie smiled as she caught this exchange, watching her son's face she knew that this was right. Margie noticed the closeness between her son and daughter-in-law that hadn't been there, even in the beginning of their marriage. It was a deeper, more intimate and satisfying kind of love between them. She now knew for a fact, that God knew exactly what he was doing all the time.

EPILOGUE

Sydney had her baby four months later. It, too, was a beautiful little baby boy. He looked so peaceful, as Sydney watched him sleep in her arms. They named him Luke Charles Davis. As Sydney sat rocking him, looking at his tiny face, she thought about how many miracles God placed into her life that she couldn't see before.

Sydney and Jeff had two more children, quite quickly after the birth of Luke. They were both boys, too. It had become a running joke that Jeff didn't want Sydney to go back to work, so that's why he kept giving her more children to take care of at home. After being pregnant for almost three years straight, Sydney finally needed a break. The other two were named Lance and Samuel. They were all one year apart and quite a handful.

The years seem to speed up after their births. Jeff and Sydney took them skiing, hiking, biking, and camping in the mountains. After the first few years of their young lives, Sydney started to lose the fear of losing one of them, although, the more active they became, the more Sydney found herself praying. They made frequent trips back home with the boys and would leave after the boys were sufficiently spoiled by Becky, Randy, and Margie.

Margie was thrilled beyond words whenever she'd visit and see how handsome they were all becoming. They had an innocence that came from having loving and caring parents that she wished that she would have given to Jeff in his young life. She could see the pride in Jeff's face when any one of them would walk into the room, tall, handsome, and strong. They showed a respect and appreciation for their parents that most didn't. Margie was being biased, she knew, but still, there was something so much more evident in her son's family that other's sometimes lacked.

After the youngest boy, Samuel, set off for college, it seemed that time had evaporated into thin air, as Sydney let him go. As she and Jeff drove slowly away from the college, leaving him there, Jeff reached over to his wife and took her hand in his. She gave him a weak smile, as she turned her head to look out to the passenger window, silently listening to her thoughts.

Looking at his wife of thirty years and watching her face, he knew exactly how she felt. "They're going to be okay you know."

"I know they will. I . . . It's just that I was just thinking about Jacob. It's hard to believe we've spent so many years together and how far we've come in that time. I feel sad that I didn't have the faith in God, when Jacob was with us, that I do now. We both had drifted so far, that I can't imagine not having Him in our lives for even a moment of time now. I guess I just worry about our boys and hope that they will always keep Him close. The best thing that I've ever done in my life is probably the easiest thing I've ever had to do, and that was closing the distance between Him and I. I guess He was never far away, but I always thought He was."

"Yeah, you're right about that. I think in my case, I bumped right into Him. Guess He figured He was tired of watching me fumble around!" Jeff snickered.

They both chuckled as they visualized that picture.

While Sydney stared out the window, she remembered Margie's statement to her so many years ago.

Tell Him Where You Hurt